Becoming a
GREAT TEACHER
of
reading

To all the great teachers of reading who make learning to read
easy and fun for their students

Becoming a
GREAT TEACHER
of
reading

Achieving High Rapid
READING GAINS
With Powerful, Differentiated Strategies

MARIE CARBO

A JOINT PUBLICATION

CORWIN PRESS
A SAGE Publications Company
Thousand Oaks, CA 91320

NATIONAL ASSOCIATION OF ELEMENTARY SCHOOL PRINCIPALS
Serving All Elementary and Middle Level Principals

For information:

Corwin Press
A Sage Publications Company
2455 Teller Road
Thousand Oaks, California 91320
www.corwinpress.com

Sage Publications India Pvt. Ltd.
B 1/I 1 Mohan Cooperative Industrial Area
Mathura Road, New Delhi 110 044
India

Sage Publications Ltd.
1 Oliver's Yard
55 City Road
London EC1Y 1SP
United Kingdom

Sage Publications Asia-Pacific Pte. Ltd.
33 Pekin Street #02–01
Far East Square
Singapore 048763

Printed in the United States of America

Library of Congress Cataloging-in-Publication Data

Carbo, Marie.
Becoming a great teacher of reading: achieving high rapid reading gains with powerful, differentiated strategies/Marie Carbo.
    p. cm.
Includes bibliographical references and index.
ISBN-13: 978-1-4129-3641-5 (cloth)
ISBN-13: 978-1-4129-3642-2 (pbk.)
    1. Reading—United States. 2. Reading—Remedial teaching—United States. I. Title.

LB1573.C255 2007
372.41—dc22
                              2007015256

This book is printed on acid-free paper.

07   08   09   10   11   10   9   8   7   6   5   4   3   2

Acquisitions Editor:	Cathy Hernandez
Editorial Assistant:	Megan Bedell
Production Editor:	Libby Larson
Typesetter:	C&M Digitals (P) Ltd.
Proofreader:	Caryne Brown
Indexer:	Michael Ferreira
Cover Designer:	Michael Dubowe

Contents

Acknowledgments

With Special Thanks to:

Faye Zucker, who inspired me to write this book, and to Cathy Hernandez, for her many kindnesses, enthusiastic support, and good advice.

My daughter Juliet and her dad, Nick Carbo, for their unending enthusiasm and strong support for my work.

Larry Barber, retired director of research for Phi Delta Kappa, for teaching attendees at our national conferences how to design and conduct classroom research on reading styles, and for his important work on the reading styles study published by Phi Delta Kappa.

My assistant, Beth Beneville, who exhibited patience and took great care—as she always does—with the many details of this project; to my graphic designer, Isabel Tavio, for her excellent work on the book's figures; and to the staff of the National Reading Styles Institute.

All the wonderful national reading styles trainers whose enormous talents and hard work helped to translate reading styles theory into workable classroom strategies as evidenced by the photographs in this book, especially Barbara Hinds, Linda Queiruga, Kay Douglas, Lois LaShell, Freda Doxey, Jill Haney, Dotti Augustine, Bob King, Karen Floro, Kim Starks, Karen Christian, Cynthia Hernandez, Kris Kraft, and Lucy Harris.

All the reading styles superintendents, principals, and teachers whose dedication, hard work, courage, and intelligence provide models of best reading styles practices for the entire nation, especially Sherry Gorsuch, principal of O'Connor Elementary, which has served as a prototype for many model schools, and to Judy Gaspard, Robert Katulak, Nancy Sullivan, Debbie Culbreth, Pat Apfel, Kim Benton, Carolyn Kerr, Beverly Crotts, Paula Hill, Janel Sewell, Sandy Holloway, Sandra Brantley, Bill Demaree, Leigh Todd, Tamala Martin, Michael Gill, Carol Tippins, Beth Jackson, Bruce Wisowaty, Cynthia Eliser, Betty Martin, Vicki Moore, Carolyn Elkins, and Larry Otte.

The following teachers and consultants for their excellent contributions: Beverly Crotts, Accommodating Children With Learning Disabilities, ADHD, and Emotional and Behavioral Disorders, Cynthia Hernandez,

Accommodating Bilingual/LEP Children; and Rebecca Thomasson, Accommodating Gifted Children.

Special thanks to Marylyn Varriale, Janet Martin, Dorothy Henson-Parker, Joyce and Kopi Saltman, and Phyllis Kaplan. Thanks also to Susanne Aabrandt for her photo contributions and fine work in reading styles in Scandanavia.

Rita Dunn, who taught me about learning styles, served as my mentor and doctoral advisor at St. John's University, and greatly supported and encouraged my work.

And, finally, to Bob Cole, who provided encouragement and sage advice at just the right times throughout the writing of this book, as well as the brilliance of his finely tuned editing.

Publisher's Acknowledgments

Corwin Press gratefully acknowledges the contributions of the following reviewers:

Diane Barone
Professor of Literacy Studies
University of Nevada, Reno, NV

Amy Benjamin
Secondary Education Consultant
Amy Benjamin Educational Services, Fishkill, NY

Jolene Dockstader
Seventh Grade Language Arts Teacher
Jerome Middle School, Jerome, ID

Roberta Sejnost
Literacy Consultant
Kane County Regional Office of Education, Geneva, IL

About the Author

 **Marie Carbo** began her career as an elementary and learning disabilities teacher, during which time her underachieving students attained unprecedented gains in reading. Her keen sense of what students need to succeed and how to make learning enjoyable guide her eminently practical approaches—all of which have from the beginning been thoroughly grounded in research.

Award-winning research, shaped by an understanding of the demands of classroom practice, are the hallmarks of Marie's career. Her doctoral dissertation received ASCD's First National Dissertation Award, and the Carbo Reading Styles Program has been named an effective, research-based reading program that improves students' reading achievement by the National Staff Development Council, the NEA, the Education Commission of the States, the Northwest Regional Lab (sponsored by the U.S. Department of Education), and the Milken Foundation. Finally, in an ASCD *Infobrief* on reading, Marie's research was named one of the 20 most important events in reading education in the last 200 years.

Marie is the founder and executive director of the National Reading Styles Institute, which has empowered tens of thousands of educators nationwide to greatly improve reading instruction through on-site training, conferences, seminars, a Web site and a network of model schools. Over the past decade, implementation of the Carbo Reading Styles Program (CRSP) has resulted in high gains in reading achievement and motivation, especially with students in the bottom third.

Marie is the creator of the concept of reading styles, as well as the Reading Style Inventory® and the developer of the Carbo Recording Method®. She has keynoted many national conferences, as well as the National Reading Styles Conference, and has served as consultant, nationally and internationally, for the Association for Supervision and Curriculum Development (ASCD), Phi Delta Kappa, state education departments, universities, school districts, and corporations. Her work has been published in nearly every major education journal, including *The Reading Teacher, Teaching Exceptional Children, Exceptional*

Children, Phi Delta Kappan, and *Educational Leadership.* She has written three ground-breaking books, including *What Every Principal Should Know About Teaching Reading,* and is currently writing three books and designing a training program for Corwin Press.

Marie may be reached at the National Reading Styles Institute, P.O. Box 737, Syosset, NY 11791; by calling 800-331-3117; and by e-mail at marie@nrsi .com. Her Web site is www.nrsi.com.

Introduction

My students with learning disabilities really taught me how to teach reading. I still remember each and every one of them—Adam, Jeffrey, Doreen, Tommy, Larry, Georgette, Suzanne—all of them. They renewed my faith in the tenacity of the human spirit, and I am filled with respect and admiration for those children every time I think about them. And I think about them often, for they are all with me every time I write about teaching, every time I work with teachers, and whenever I visit our model schools. Those students taught me more than how to teach reading; they taught me to believe in myself as a teacher, to persevere, and not to accept theories that hurt children.

My own great lessons began thirty years ago with the first twenty students on my caseload. They were basically sweet, good children who just couldn't read. The first- and second-graders in this group couldn't read at all, and the older students were struggling and stumbling on first- and second-grade levels. There they were in their regular classrooms, trying desperately to look as if they knew what was going on. How could they? They couldn't read most of the words in their rooms, their textbooks—much of anything. My heart went out to them, but they needed more than that. They needed me to teach them to read.

My awakening to what these children needed didn't happen overnight, I can tell you. I worked and worked with each of them, trying to figure out the best ways of reaching them. Then it came to me: their strengths! The best way to reach these frustrated children was the way in which all children learn best: through their strengths. My teaching was never the same from that moment on. That powerful realization caused me to look at all students and all classrooms in a new and different light.

Take the class with which I had just begun to work as my first example. Who were these kids, really? What could they do? And what did they have trouble doing? I realized then that these children were dropouts from the strong phonics program used in my district. They couldn't learn phonics because they had auditory dyslexia—extreme auditory deficiencies that made them incapable of learning much, if any, phonics. So, all of them failed phonics in the early grades, and didn't learn to read. But their problems with schools—and with reading—didn't end in the early grades. Throughout the grades, they were given remedial phonics. It never stopped, until we worked together. They were, as we would all learn together, very capable of learning to read.

Please understand: The issue wasn't phonics. The issue was, and is, creating the right match between students' strengths and the best way of teaching them. Phonics isn't a goal; it's one method of teaching children to read. The overarching goal—the reason we teach any child to read—is to create a person who loves reading, who reads to learn, and who will be a lifelong reader and learner. That's our business. Phonics is simply one way of reaching that enormously important goal. There are many, many other methods. The key is matching the method with the student and his or her strengths.

Unfortunately, that way of thinking was counter to the prevailing wisdom thirty years ago, when I began teaching children with learning disabilities. I had to become a maverick if my heart and integrity were to survive. So I did. I soon discovered, however, that I was a maverick with lots of company. In my doctoral coursework, I encountered the field of learning styles and was able to put my work with reading into a larger (and very well-researched) context. Later, the field of brain-based learning solved another piece of the reading puzzle.

In the meantime, my students learned to read. And I learned the power of doing the obvious—which is always to look first at students' strengths and at their style of learning.

For instance, when I realized Georgette's major problem was a memory deficit (she was repeating second grade and could only read her name), I created a simple method of tape recording words and stories for her. She learned 31 words in the first month we worked together.

Since all of my students couldn't learn with phonics, I taught them to write stories using a word-tracing technique. They liked it and it helped them. I knew that the children were still struggling a lot when they read, and they hated the low-level reading materials they had to read, so I devised a method of recording slowly, and I recorded just small amounts so they could re-listen enough to learn the material. That method enabled me to stretch them into higher and more interesting materials.

One of the grandest days of all was when Tommy—a sixth-grader who read on a first-grade level—read a portion of *Charlotte's Web* that I had recorded with this method. His reading was fluent and smooth. I watched Tommy change before my eyes. For the first time, I felt the hope he had in his heart that he would learn to read. He knew I felt it. It was a glorious moment for both of us, just glorious. Tommy gained 1.3 years in reading in just three months, all of it while working with the recordings that I had made for him of *Charlotte's Web*.

They are all here with me as I finish this introduction, for they are always with me in my heart. I hope that this book helps you all to put your children first always, teach them through their strengths, experiment with the strategies in this book, and, first and foremost, never lose faith that your students can learn to read. It doesn't have to be step-by-step. They can and will make great leaps forward. Listen to their interests, honor their strengths, and you and they will accomplish what seem like miracles. You can do it. I know you can.

1

Believe That All Students Can Learn

You have the power within you to become a great teacher of reading, to change your students' lives, to affect generations. When you teach your students to love reading and to read well, they in turn can help their parents and siblings—and, eventually, their own children—learn to read. As you forge links to literacy with your students, you empower them to become all that they can be, to contribute to society, to become good citizens. Great teachers release and nurture their students' natural power to learn, and they believe that all of their students can learn to read well.

THE GRAND PURPOSE OF THIS BOOK

The purpose of this book is a grand one: to help you to become a great teacher of reading. If you already are such a teacher, then this book's purpose is to enhance your greatness. Your first and most important step toward becoming a great teacher of reading is to keep your own power strong. Why? Because there has never been a more challenging time to be a teacher. You are standing on the front lines of a battle for our children's future. Consider these facts (which are presented in greater detail in Appendix B):

• Research tells us that each year reading for pleasure declines (Dillon, 2005a), that less than one-third of our students in Grades 4, 8, and 12 are reading at or above their grade level (Dillon, 2005b), and that boys' dislike for school keeps rising. After fourth grade, boys fall far behind girls in reading; by twelfth grade, smaller and smaller percentages of boys are attending college due to their low levels of literacy (Newkirk, 2003).

• Even more foreboding, the literacy levels of our college graduates are falling. Only 31% of our college graduates demonstrated reading proficiency on the National Assessment of Adult Literacy given in 2003 by the Department of Education, compared to 40% in 1992. And 14% of college graduates scored at the basic level, which demonstrates an ability to read and understand only short, commonplace texts (Dillon, 2005c).

• Despite the fact that *little to no research* supports the use of large amounts of worksheets or skill sheets to teach reading, the number of worksheets has *grown* since 1985. (One likely reason is that consumable workbooks bring in huge amounts of revenue for basal programs and others.) Some basal programs have 1,000 reading worksheets or more just for first grade—about six worksheets every school day! Six worksheets could take a student one and a half to two hours to complete. Is it any wonder that, year after year, reading for pleasure continues to decrease throughout the grades?

• A high percentage of U.S. students appear to be performing at the proficient reading level on their state exams, but a very low percentage perform at that level on the more valid and accurate National Assessment of Educational Progress (NAEP). For example, 87% of Georgia fourth graders scored at the proficient level on their state exam, but only 26% of them scored at the proficient level on the NAEP (Ravitch, 2005). Easy state tests are extremely dangerous; they make it appear that students are doing well when they're not, lulling the public into keeping the reading instruction that exists, rather than looking into why their students are actually doing so poorly (see Figure 1.1).

• It's not just the enormous overemphasis on the big test administered at the end of the school year that creates a barrier to learning. It's also the yearlong, endless testing and test practice, the continual fear of failure, and the high levels of stress—these all have a devastatingly negative effect on learning. While small amounts of stress can increase motivation, large doses cause fear, decrease motivation, and reduce the ability of students to think and perform at high levels (Sprenger, 1999). Yet we continue to go round and round, getting nowhere. There's no time for reading enjoyment because students have to prepare for tests. Students have to prepare for reading tests because scores are low. Scores are low because students don't read. Students don't read because they don't enjoy reading. And on and on and on.

• The first cousin of overtesting is an overemphasis on skills teaching. And yet few of the hundreds of skills and subskills have been validated as being necessary for children to become good readers! In fact, as I'll demonstrate throughout this book, at-risk readers who have made great leaps in reading ability have spent most of their time reading books and short stories they enjoy with the aid of modeling methods, with only small amounts of time spent on reading skills. Unreasonable increases in skill work and testing invariably result in less voluntary reading and lowered student motivation (Foertsch, 1992).

All of us could agree that these are serious problems. But what are today's solutions to these problems? Unfortunately, instead of counteracting the lack of interest in reading by making learning to read easy and fun, we keep testing our students more and more; developing longer and more complex reading manuals for teachers to wade through; increasing the use of boring worksheets; requiring the teaching and re-teaching of a multitude of reading skills that are often unnecessary for many students; ignoring what our students say they want to read; and teaching to the tests. In other words, much of what is being done today to improve literacy disregards important research in reading, learning styles, and how the brain learns. These so-called solutions are likely to worsen the reading problem and increase the number of bored, stressed students who dislike reading—exactly what we don't want.

BEGINNING OUR JOURNEY TOWARD GREATNESS

Keeping all this in mind, let's begin our journey toward greatness together and see how we can help all students learn to read with ease and enjoyment. Reading enjoyment is of primary importance because we know that students who love to read tend to read a great deal, improve their reading steadily, perform well on reading tests—and become lifelong readers (Guthrie, Shafter, & Huang, 2001).

Today, many of our students dislike or even hate reading. James was one of those students. Let's see what we can learn from his true story.

James was a poor, black, male Mississippi ninth grader reading four years below his grade level. What we'll learn from his story can be applied to all grades. As ninth grade begins, this is what he said to his reading teacher, Lori Lambert:

> **August 1995**: I hate to read. You will never make me read, and I will never read!

At the time, James was 16 and felt he had no future. No matter how hard he had tried, each year his textbooks became more difficult, and he couldn't catch up. Deep inside, he felt scared and stupid. Outwardly, he showed only anger. Toward the end of ninth grade, this is what James said quietly to his teacher.

> **May 1996:** I read every night before I go to bed. I especially like to read *Sports Illustrated*. Before this class I hated reading. Now I want to read everything that interests me, especially sports.

With the help of the key reading strategies you'll find in this book, James immediately started reading better. In fact, he enjoyed reading so much that he began to read every night before bed. In just six months, he gained two and a half years in reading comprehension, rising from a 5.1 to a 7.6 reading level. It had taken James 10 agonizing, failure-filled years to gain only five years in reading. Yet in ninth grade, he gained nearly half that amount in only *six months.* Not only was he able to leap forward in reading about eight times faster than he had in 10 years of schooling, in ninth grade James became a confident reader.

What Worked for James and Why

James's ninth-grade reading program differed sharply from traditional reading programs for at-risk readers, which often place a heavy emphasis on reading skills and worksheets. Such programs have invariably widened the gap between good and poor readers at all grade levels (Allington, 1983, 1991; Applebee, Langer, & Mullis, 1988; Johnston & Allington, 1991; Pearson, 1992). In the reading lab that James attended, skill work was minimized. Instead, James learned about his "reading style" (his learning style for reading). He learned what his natural strengths were and how to study and make use of those strengths in all his classes (Chapters 4 and 5 discuss this topic in detail). He spent about 90% of his time in the lab reading high-interest stories that he chose, and only about 10% of his time on skill work directly related to those stories. The large amount of reading done by James helped him to increase his reading fluency, vocabulary, and comprehension (Nagy, Anderson, & Herman, 1987; Stanovich, 2000).

Most important, James advanced quickly because the stories in the lab were all recorded in small amounts with a special, slow pace and chunked phrases that enabled him to follow along in a story easily and learn the words. (This method is described in Chapter 7.) After repeated listenings of a story, James would meet with his teacher, read a portion of the story aloud, discuss and summarize the story, and then answer a few comprehension and vocabulary questions. His reading program was challenging, fun, and fail-safe—all critically important factors for maximum learning to take place, according to current brain research (Armstrong 1998; Caine, Caine, McClintic, & Klimek, 2005; Jensen, 1998a, 1998b; Sprenger, 1999, 2003).

For the first time, James was able to relax and enjoy reading. As we saw in James's second quote above, some of his favorite stories came from *Sports Illustrated,* which is written on about a tenth-grade reading level (even though he reached only a 7.6 reading level by the end of ninth grade). The specialized recordings of the stories enabled James's teacher to continually stretch him with higher- and higher-level reading materials in which he was deeply interested. That stretching process was an important factor in his gaining 2.5 years in reading in only six months.

What was *not* done in James's reading program was also important. He was not continually tested, and he did not spend time practicing to take

Figure 1.1   A Sampling of NAEP Versus State Scores for Percent of Students Reading at the Proficient Level

State	NAEP	State Test
Georgia (Gr. 4)	26%	83%
Alabama (Gr. 4)	22%	83%
Texas (Gr. 8)	26%	83%
N. Carolina (Gr. 8)	26%	88%
Tennessee (Gr. 8)	27%	88%

Compared to the National Assessment of Educational Progress (NAEP), results of many state tests indicate much higher percentages of proficient readers.

Figure 1.2   James's ninth-grade classmates at work in their Reading Lab with specially recorded books and stories.

SOURCE: Photo courtesy of Ed Mayo Jr. High, Moss Point, MS.

any tests. James was tested only twice—once in November at the inception of the program, and once in May at the end of the program. The Gates-MacGinitie Achievement Test was group administered to determine the reading growth of the 45 students who attended the reading lab; they made an average gain in reading comprehension of 2.2 years in six months. From November to May, word counts were not done, stories that bored the students were not used (the students' interests determined most of the reading material in the lab), few worksheets were used, and important reading time was not wasted. Note: *After* highly at-risk readers make substantial reading gains, then some reading materials outside of their strong interests can be introduced.

The "right" reading work for any student should result in increased reading achievement and motivation and *increased reading for pleasure.* The work should be interesting and exciting, thereby tapping into the most powerful kind of memory, emotional memory (Jensen, 1998a, 1998b; Sprenger, 1999). It should make use of the students' reading style strengths and preferences. In short, learning to read should be easy and fun. *When it's difficult and boring, it's invariably the wrong work!*

Beating the Odds and Changing Lives

For a moment, let's move the clock back. In the late spring of 1995, James's teacher, Lori Lambert, attended one of our trainings. On her first break, she called her principal and requested that he assign her the lowest readers in their school for the next school year. She was assigned students who were reading three to seven years below grade level. By the end of that school year, the headline in the local newspaper, the *Mississippi Press,* read: "Reading program *changes* students' lives" (Anglin, 1996; Figure 1.3).

What was accomplished in just six months with Lambert's high-risk, older students is all too rare today. Research tells us that once students fall far behind in reading by third grade, they rarely catch up. By the time they reach middle school or high school (if they stay in school that long), their chances of closing the gap are extremely slim. Yet Lambert's students made average gains of 2.2 years in reading comprehension in just six months (Figure 1.4). Not only were their reading gains extremely high, the reading program was easy and fun for them. The students felt little stress, could choose what they wanted to read, spent most of their time reading and enjoying what they read, and were able to move to higher-level reading materials quickly with the aid of the modeling reading methods and special recordings described in Chapters 6 and 7.

GREAT TEACHING AND IMPRESSIVE RESULTS K–12

Use of the strategies in this book has helped good teachers of reading to become great teachers. These teachers demonstrate repeatedly that even

Figure 1.3   By the end of the school year, this was the headline in
The Mississippi Press.

SOURCE: Photo by William Colgin, Staff Photographer, *The Mississippi Press.*

Figure 1.4   Reading Gains of At-Risk Ninth Graders in Six Months

% of Students	Reading Gains in Years
25%	3.0 to 6.6
50%	1.0 to 2.9
10%	.6 to .9
15%	>.6

**The average gain in reading comprehension
for 45 students was 2.2 years on the Gates-MacGinitie
Achievement Test.**

the most at-risk students can achieve, behave well, and surpass academic expectations. When teachers have implemented the strategies in this book at a high level schoolwide, visitors sense a feeling of joy, humor, vitality, playfulness, and a strong focus on learning. Here are results from some of our model districts, schools, and reading labs:

Bledsoe County (Bledsoe, TN, K–12, rural Appalachia, low socioeconomic). One of the early success stories came from Bledsoe County (Snyder, 1994). In the mid-1980s, Bledsoe schools averaged a stanine score of only three in reading—not unusual for a rural school district in a poverty area. After three years of reading styles strategies, Bledsoe schools gained two stanines in reading, equaling state and national averages, and received the Governor's Award for Educational Excellence.

Marion Elementary School (Marion, MI, PreK–5, rural, 99% White, one-third of families have no phones, high unemployment, 61% free or reduced lunch). In 2001, 42.1% of the fourth graders at Marion Elementary scored at the proficient reading level on their state test (the MEAP). After three years of reading styles, the percentage of fourth graders scoring at the proficient level rose to 87% in 2005, and to 95% in 2006.

Ocean City Elementary School (PreK–5, Ft. Walton Beach, 70% low socioeconomic, 30% ESE). After implementing reading styles, the school closed the reading gap between their White students (from 65% proficient in 2003 to 73% proficient in 2005) and African American students (from 50% proficient in 2003 to 72% in 2005), and narrowed the reading gap for students who were economically disadvantaged or who had learning disabilities.

O'Connor Elementary School (Victoria, TX, PreK–5, 74% Hispanic, low socioeconomic, schoolwide Title I). In 1993, after one year of reading styles, O'Connor rose from 19% to 80% of its students passing their state reading test. By 2006, over 97% of O'Connor's 500-plus students passed math, reading, and writing at all tested grade levels.

West Amory Elementary School (Amory, MS, PreK–2, rural, 58% free or reduced lunch, schoolwide Title I). After three years of reading styles, in 2002 West Amory was one of three Title I schools to achieve the highest NCE gains in Mississippi (their students gained 38.5 NCEs in reading in three years), and won the IRA Distinguished Title I School Award.

West Haverstraw Elementary School (North Rockland, NY, suburban, PreK–6, 79% free or reduced lunch, 63% limited English proficiency). Between 2003 and 2006, West Haverstraw Elementary used reading styles strategies and rose from a school "In Need of Improvement," to the "Exemplary List of Most Improved Schools," to a "High Performing/Gap Closing" school in Language Arts and Math (New York state's highest rating). During that same period, discipline referrals and suspensions dropped by 50%, according to Assistant Superintendent Robert Katulak.

Immokalee High School Reading Lab (Collier County, Naples, FL, Grades 10–12, 94% minority). After only seven weeks, 21 regular English students gained two years in reading comprehension, and 23 ESE students gained seven months during that same period on the Gates-MacGinitie Reading

Figure 1.5   Two third graders work at a bulletin board/learning station. They are separating the events from several stories, and then sequencing the events.

SOURCE: Photo courtesy of O'Connor Elementary School, Victoria, TX.

Achievement Test. By the second year (2003), Bridgett Morris, reading lab teacher, wrote:

> We are bursting at the seams for this term. There are about 200 students utilizing the lab—all English classes, the FCAT skills class, and some ESE classes. We've also created a movable Carbo Lab for the ESOL students at lower levels. Things are going great!

Grand Caillou Middle School (Houma, LA, Grades 4–8, 85% free or reduced lunch, 54% minority, 11% migrant). Grand Caillou's graduates outperformed their more privileged counterparts in their district, and the district's high school teachers reported that "Grand Caillou graduates stand out. They like to read more than other kids, take more interest in their classes, and know what they need to do to learn." The school was so outstanding that Grand Caillou principal Judy Gaspard became the only American invited to present at the United Nations Conference of 2002. Gaspard was asked to join an international panel that honored innovative programs that promote knowledge, human rights, and peace education.

Besides high academic gains, Gaspard (personal communication, June 18, 2006) reported sharply decreased aggressive student behavior. She described this dramatic change:

Before the program there were two to three fights a day. In these fights the kids physically injured each other. After the first year of the program we had an average of two fights a month, which mainly involved words of anger. The third year we may have had a fight every two months, usually between students new to our school. Then fights became a thing of the past. Students were talking to us about their problems before it became a fight. The *students* were not accepting fistfights as a way of settling their differences.

Figure 1.6   Using the strategies in this book, O'Connor Elementary rose from 19% to 80% of their students passing their state reading test. By 2001, 98% passed, and O'Connor received an "Exemplary" rating from the Texas Dept. of Education. O'Connor maintained those high scores through its last testing in 2006.

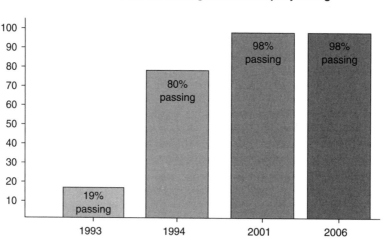

From 19% to 99% Passing and an Exemplary Rating

HOW TEACHERS PERCEIVE AT-RISK READERS

Great teaching often begins with major changes in how we perceive our students. So how do teachers perceive at-risk readers? I've asked about 4,500 teachers to describe the behavior of their at-risk readers. Teachers' responses spill forth rapidly, and their most common answers are decidedly negative. Their at-risk readers, they say, are angry (the most common response), frustrated, resentful, lazy. They are class clowns, withdrawn; they act out. The list goes on until I stop the activity.

Figure 1.7   Teachers' Descriptors for At-Risk Readers

angry*	defeated
frustrated	scared
withdrawn	hopeless
unmotivated	slow
feel stupid	explosive
disruptive	embarrassed
distracted	hyperactive
unhappy	off-task
disorganized	impulsive
sad	need attention
hyperactive	short attention span
don't care	intimidated
class clowns	lost

Most common responses of approximately 4,500 teachers from across the United States between 1998 and 2005.
* "Angry" was the most common response.

My next question is: How much class time do you spend dealing with the negative behavior of at-risk readers? The most common estimates from teachers are a whopping 50% to 90% of their class time. Apparently, teachers spend an enormous amount of their teaching time thinking about and trying to improve or "handle" the negative behaviors of their at-risk readers, especially at the middle and high school levels. Undoubtedly, this problem with behavior has contributed to the use of scripted, rigid reading programs—precisely what most teachers and at-risk readers don't need.

My last question is: How do you feel about what you're accomplishing with your at-risk readers? Here the answers are slow at first, and then they come forth in spurts. Many teachers say they feel frustrated, tired, ineffective, inadequate, sad, hopeless, burned out. Some of their answers mirror the words they use to describe their students!

They also say that contributing to their problems are the rigidly mandated hundreds of skills at each grade level, the countless piles of paperwork that distance them from their students, the endless test preparation, and the never-ending tests throughout the school year—all working against student engagement and achievement.

These teachers are correct! The pressure on teachers today is enormous. But most teachers still say that they became teachers to make a difference. They want to do a good job, they want to be excited about teaching, and they're willing to work hard to help their students.

HERE'S THE GOOD NEWS

The good news is that the often sad, fearful, angry behaviors of at-risk readers subside when these students experience success. For that to happen, reading programs need to be easy and engaging, with large doses of brain-friendly strategies that are successful, respectful of student differences, and fail-safe. Then learning accelerates, and students become excited about and interested in what they're learning.

Figure 1.8   Style of At-Risk Reader

Highly Tactile	Needs Mobility
Highly Kinesthetic	Prefers Choices
Global	Needs Structure
Prefers Group Work	

Remember that constant failure is poisonous to both students and teachers. It causes high levels of stress, and stress dulls the mind and creates anger and fear. Caine et al. (2005) explain this phenomenon, stating: "Excessive stress actually short-circuits the brain/mind and reduces the ability of people to engage their own higher-order capacities" (p. 30). Excessive frustration and stress sabotage students' abilities, make them feel stupid, and often lead to unacceptable conduct. Psychologists explain that many students prefer to be regarded as "behavior problems" rather than as slow or stupid.

On the other hand, positive emotions have the opposite effect. They motivate young people and create excitement (Jensen, 1998a). The powerful teaching strategies in this book have helped students to read substantially better and to feel smart and capable. One visible side effect has been diminished negative behavior. And that enables teachers to spend more time teaching, use more effective strategies, and enjoy teaching. *Success breeds more success.*

THE POWER OF TEACHING
TO STUDENTS' STRENGTHS

We all need to perceive students in terms of their strengths rather than their disabilities. Unfortunately, many teachers do not teach to students' strengths—and that can be heard clearly in their descriptions of their students: They can't sit still, can't hear sounds. They're dyslexic, get bored easily, disrupt others. They're lazy—and on and on. These behaviors are often the result of boring reading materials and inappropriate teaching methods that don't nurture our students or engage their interests, don't provide appropriate modeling, don't compensate for their weaknesses, and don't teach to their strengths.

This is especially true for at-risk readers who tend as a group to be global, tactile/kinesthetic learners. These youngsters benefit from high-interest, challenging reading materials, structured choices, powerful modeling of texts, hands-on skill work, and opportunities for mobility and working in groups (Figure 1.9). Many students are at risk because they don't receive the kind of instruction and materials that would enable them to learn easily. The rest of the chapters in this book provide strategies that accommodate the interests and strengths of all your students, especially at-risk readers.

Figure 1.9   Powerful Strategies for At-Risk Readers

- Focus on comprehension, enjoyment, interests, and learning strengths.
- Provide choices of high-interest reading materials.
- Use reading methods that accommodate students' strengths.
- Use powerful assisted reading methods.
- Provide sufficient repetition.
- Practice skills with hands-on games.
- Reduce visual dyslexia with colored overlays.
- Make learning to read easy, enjoyable, and fail-safe.

YOU CAN CHANGE AND SAVE LIVES

Even though James was angry and belligerent at the beginning of ninth grade, his teacher was able to see beyond his outward behavior. Her confidence and belief in his abilities as a learner and in her own ability to teach him persuaded James and his classmates to try and provided the strong motivation they needed to succeed. Let's not forget the enormous pain and suffering caused to James and his classmates during their first 10 years of school, and the incalculable loss of all the information they might have learned had they been able to read their textbooks along the way, as well as the joy they should have experienced by reading books that excited and interested them.

We know that risk is pervasive and terribly dangerous. Being an at-risk reader places a student at risk of other factors. Compared to average and good readers, students with low reading scores are three times more likely to fail their courses, four times more likely to be referred for special education, twice as likely to be absent excessively, more likely to be retained, suspended, drop out, do jail time, and even to commit suicide (Frymier et al., 1992; Kozol, 2005). According to the editor of *Jails*, about 80%–85% of prisoners read at a second- to third-grade reading level. Since there are fewer and fewer jobs in this society for low-level readers, those who can't find work have a greater risk of committing a crime and going to jail.

Great teachers *change* the lives of their students by enabling them to perform well in school. Ultimately, they provide their students with a better chance to obtain a good job and live a better life. They decrease the crime rate and the number of suicides. The most important gift teachers can give to their students is to teach them to read well, and to make this process so easy, enjoyable, and fail-safe that they become lifelong readers.

RESEARCH-SUPPORTED STRATEGIES

More than 20 years of research clearly indicates that when students are taught through their reading styles—their strongest learning pathways—their ability to learn to read accelerates (Barber, Carbo, & Thomasson, 1998; Bradsby, Wise, Mundell, & Haas, 1992; Brooks, 1991; Carbo Reading Styles Program, 2000; Hodgin & Wooliscroft, 1997; LaShell, 1986; Oglesby & Suter, 1995; Skipper, 1997; Snyder, 1994, 1997).

All of the strategies in this book were developed for and are used extensively in the Carbo Reading Styles Program (CRSP), which has been identified and listed as a research-based language arts program by the Education Commission of the States, the National Staff Development Council, the Northwest Regional Lab (funded by the U.S. Department of Education), the Milken Foundation, and the New England Comprehensive Center. See Appendix C for more information and research.

IN THE NEXT CHAPTER . . .

In Chapter 2, I'll lay out the 12 guiding principles that pave the way for success in teaching reading to any students, anytime, anywhere. Please remember: Our aim, as great teachers of reading, is to create lifelong readers who read because they *enjoy* it and comprehend at high levels!

2

Understand These Guiding Principles

In this chapter, I lay out the guiding principles underlying the powerful, differentiated strategies that will be described in detail throughout this book. These principles are guideposts on the way to great teaching. They are based on research in reading, learning styles, reading styles, and brain behavior.

First of all, though, before the principles, we need to stop doing what isn't working for our students. Many teachers are distressed by the huge amounts of paperwork, test practice, skill teaching, and the need to discipline students who are bored by the stories and worksheets they are given. If you are one of those teachers, take heart. Expert opinion is on your side.

Here is what reading experts recommend you decrease in your teaching (Flippo, 1998; Reutzel & Smith, 2004). These practices tend to make learning to read difficult: too many worksheets, especially for struggling readers; boring stories; skills taught in isolation; stories with highly controlled vocabularies; exclusive teaching of phonics; a focus on skill instruction instead of comprehension; written book reports on every book or story read; "round robin reading;" and, last, following most teacher editions faithfully instead of responding to the needs of your students.

Now, let's move on to the 12 guiding principles.

PRINCIPLE #1: LEARNING TO READ SHOULD BE EASY AND FUN

When the process of learning to read is laborious, embarrassing, and difficult, students are likely to dislike and avoid reading. Like James in Chapter 1, many struggling readers feel stupid because they can't read well; they become angry and resentful.

All students need to be interested in and emotionally involved in the stories they're reading. Young children and struggling readers need sufficient modeling of their stories before they are asked to read aloud. They often need to learn through multiple modalities, and they benefit from small-group work. Too much skill work and too many worksheets are barriers to their success. Large reading gains happen for most students when student engagement is high, stress is reduced, reading is modeled if necessary, and much of the learning is activity based.

Recommended Strategies

- If needed, reduce the amount of worksheets and skill work. Make reading easy and fun! Too much paperwork wastes precious time.
- Schedule a variety of people to read to your students (other teachers, authors, the principal, family members, older students). Students of all ages need to see and hear people *enjoying* reading, and then experience that enjoyment themselves.
- Provide time for students to read with friends if they wish—including cross-age or cross-classroom friends.
- Allow students to practice passages before reading aloud. Reading aloud in a hesitant, stumbling manner in front of classmates is *the number one worst memory* of adults who were struggling readers as children. Struggling readers, in particular, should *never* be asked to read aloud unless they have been helped with sufficient modeling techniques, allowed to practice, and want to read aloud.

PRINCIPLE #2: IT'S NATURAL FOR CHILDREN TO ENJOY READING AND TO BE MOTIVATED TO READ

It's the job of schools to make reading enjoyable and motivating, to bring out students' natural interests and curiosity, and to encourage new interests. When reading connects with students' emotions, when their deepest interests are tapped, these emotions activate many storage areas in the brain (Sprenger, 1999). Highly motivated students become more responsible about reading and are more likely to practice reading regularly. And, since learning accelerates when students are relaxed, open, and receptive (Armstrong, 1998; Jensen, 1998), it's also important to provide them with comfortable environments.

Recommended Strategies

- Provide a relaxing, literature-rich reading environment. Design cozy, inviting reading centers with lamps, rugs, soft chairs, and pillows. Most readers prefer to read in an informal setting. Teachers of older students often make available to their students carpet squares (for sitting on the floor), and a few folding chairs.
- Provide a wide range of reading choices. Ask students about their interests and stock class libraries accordingly.
- Have on hand lots of short books and short stories on topics that students want to read about. Short stories enable you to provide many choices for struggling readers. Since at-risk readers can finish short stories quickly, they can move forward to higher and higher reading levels at a good rate. Add longer books as students are ready for them, find them highly interesting, and want to read them.
- Encourage students to recommend what they've read and enjoyed. Post a blank sheet of paper with the words "I RECOMMEND" at the top, with three vertical columns below that title. The student writes his or her name, the name of the story or book being recommended, and the reason for the recommendation.
- Form book clubs that meet on a regular basis (Adventure Club, Mystery Club, Sci-Fi Club, Sports Club, and so on). Allow students to create bulletin boards that reflect their reading interests.

PRINCIPLE #3: CHILDREN LEARN FROM MODELING

Throughout the grades, research tells us, students are increasingly less motivated to read, and reading for pleasure declines. Make the time to read to your students. The enthusiasm, interest, and delight you exhibit when you read aloud to your students is contagious. So much teaching time is wasted preparing students for tests that many teachers say that they don't have time to read to their students, talk about books, or recommend books. Yet these activities are critically important for *all* students—especially struggling readers, many of whom enter school having been read to very little and therefore lacking familiarity with the structure and vocabulary of written language.

Recommended Strategies

- If students have been read to very little, set aside 10–15 minutes twice daily during the school day to read aloud to them. For older students, read aloud for about 5–10 minutes of a class period.
- Assign an older, good reader to read aloud to younger students, or to small groups of struggling readers. When struggling readers master

a story and want to read it aloud to younger students, make arrangements for them to do so.

- Place stories, poems, information, and word lists on the chalkboard, overheads, or large charts. Using a pointer or yardstick, point just above the words or phrases and choral-read them with your students a few minutes daily.
- For nonfluent readers, try the echo method (Chapter 6). Read aloud a short passage from a textbook or a storybook once or twice, at a somewhat slow pace, while students follow along in their own books. Then have the students choral-read the passage back to you. Start with just a sentence or two and work up to longer amounts. Note: The purpose of this activity is to familiarize the student with the vocabulary and information in the textbook. Textbooks are not generally of high interest and are, therefore, not recommended for teaching students to read, except in rare cases of high student interest.

PRINCIPLE #4: STRETCHING STUDENTS WITH HIGH-LEVEL READING MATERIALS INCREASES READING ABILITY

In Chapter 1, James was able to read high-level reading materials that thoroughly engaged him and affirmed to him that he was progressing at a fast pace in reading. Special recordings enabled James to read back stories that were written *years* above his reading level. It was that steady stretching process that brought his reading level up so high and so quickly.

Stretching occurs too rarely in most reading programs. If we don't stretch our students with materials written at higher and higher levels, many of them make only small gains in reading each year, falling further and further behind. This stretching process needs to be done so that students are challenged but not defeated. And let's remember that many struggling readers are global learners who need exciting, motivating, well-written materials to do their best. We all want to read materials in which we're interested. For struggling readers, high-interest reading material is even more crucial.

Recommended Strategies

- Read aloud challenging materials often and ask thought-provoking questions, such as predicting or interpreting the behavior of story characters.
- Have teams of students challenge one another with high-level reading questions that they create.

- Learn the assisted reading methods in Chapter 6. These methods will enable you to use higher-level reading materials with your students immediately.
- Stretch students with the special recording method described in Chapter 7. This method increases fluency, word recognition, vocabulary, and comprehension in short periods of time. Note: Permission from copyright holders is required before recording. See the end of Chapter 7 for a brief discussion of copyright laws.

PRINCIPLE # 5: LITERACY-RICH ENVIRONMENTS INCREASE READING MOTIVATION

Now that we have stretched students with higher-level reading materials and provided the modeling methods and special recordings that help them to read and understand these materials, we need to create a reading environment that engages students. That means a display of many reading materials, both nonfiction and fiction, depending on the students' interests.

Use posters, charts, book covers, student drawings, and special bulletin board displays to expose students to more and more kinds of reading. Research tells us that older students, especially boys, want to read series books, sports and car magazines, and comic books, so include some of that reading material as well. Make your classroom or reading lab inviting and exciting for children.

Recommended Strategies

- Identify students' interests through questionnaires and interviews. Provide as many reading materials as possible based on their interests.
- Organize recorded short stories in folders or plastic envelopes along with their audiotapes or CDs, for easy access by students. Or, place packets of stapled stories with their recordings in a central location. Remember, most students progress faster with short stories and short books because they can finish quickly and move up to more difficult reading material faster.
- Label objects for those who need it, and post written charts that interest the students. Charts and pictures about favorite books, stories, and characters stimulate student interest.
- Provide a comfortable reading area with rugs, pillows, and soft chairs.
- Include an array of reading materials, such as poetry, fiction and nonfiction, magazines, specially recorded storybooks, comics, newspaper articles, stories written by students, reading games, software—all based, as much as possible, on students' interests.

Figure 2.1   Standing at a bookshelf and surrounded by print, this student builds vocabulary words from Scrabble game tiles.

SOURCE: Courtesy of Stemley Road Elementary School, Talladega County, AL.

PRINCIPLE #6: GOOD READERS SPEND TIME PRACTICING READING

Let's assume that we have motivated students to read. They have heard many excellent and inspiring reading models, both live and recorded. They're working in literacy-rich environments, and we have made the process of learning to read easy and fun. What's the next step?

Practice, practice, practice. There is a strong correlation between amount of reading for pleasure and reading growth (Allington, 2001; Anderson, 1996; Krashen, 1993). Yet most American children spend very little time reading anything at all. As they move up through the grades, they enjoy reading less, read voluntarily less, and use the library less. In order to become good readers, our students need to spend a great deal of time reading, especially reading materials that they enjoy. Students learn to read by *reading*. Practice helps to improve reading comprehension and vocabulary; and there is no doubt that practice will also help to raise test scores.

Recommended Strategies

- Set aside specific, uninterrupted reading periods during the school day.
- During quiet reading times, like sustained silent reading, provide special recordings of high-interest stories and books for your struggling readers. After youngsters listen to the recordings, conference with them so they can read a portion to you and discuss what they read.
- If you have struggling readers on approximately the same reading level, have them listen to a portion of a recorded story a few times at a listening center. Then work with them as a group to summarize the story, discuss it, and read back parts of it.
- Sell affordable books.
- Encourage students to take books home to read.
- Sponsor book exchanges that allow students to exchange books.

PRINCIPLE #7: BALANCED LITERACY INSTRUCTION HELPS STUDENTS TO MAKE IMPORTANT CONNECTIONS

Many reading experts recommend balanced reading instruction, especially in the early grades (Cunningham & Hall, 1998; Hiebert & Raphael, 1998; Pressley, 1998, 2001). This type of teaching helps students to understand and make connections between the skill work they do and the language arts—listening, speaking, reading, and writing. Outstanding teachers have been found to use all or many of the strategies recommended in this section (Pressley, 1998).

Recommended Strategies

- Teach phonemics and phonics directly, and connect these teachings to all the language arts.
- Provide direct instruction in comprehension by modeling and demonstrating how skilled, fluent reading is accomplished. Discuss stories with children, use think-alouds, and emphasize high-level questions.

- Use story discussions to elaborate and clarify student understandings, and to enable students to express their emotions and feelings.
- Provide time for students to write about what they've read, at least weekly. If this procedure causes stress for some students, have them dictate what they want to write to you, and then read what you've written. As confidence improves, encourage students to do more of their own writing.
- Allow students time to choose what they want to read from a variety of reading materials and levels of difficulty.
- Provide time for and encourage extensive reading of informational and narrative texts.

PRINCIPLE #8: PROVIDE ASSISTANCE FOR ENGLISH LANGUAGE LEARNERS

A recent review of the research on teaching reading to Spanish-speaking students indicates that paired bilingual instruction is more effective than English immersion models. In the paired bilingual model, reading instruction both in Spanish and in English is provided at different times of the day (Slavin & Cheung, 2004).

The authors explained one of the primary benefits of this model:

> Rather than confusing children, as some have feared, reading instruction in a familiar language may serve as a bridge to success in English, as phonemic awareness, decoding, sound blending, and generic comprehension strategies clearly transfer among languages that use phonetic orthographies, such as Spanish, French, and English. (p. 43)

In this section, we will look at different kinds of bridges that can be created within the regular classroom to help ELL students improve both their spoken English and ability to read English.

Recommended Strategies

- Use volunteers to work one-on-one or with small groups of ELL students. Volunteers can select books and other materials to conduct read-alouds, shared readings, and shared writings.
- Use the echo reading method with pairs of students (one fluent in English and one learning English). The two students take turns reading in this manner. First the student who is fluent in English reads a sentence; then the ELL student reads back the same sentence, and so on. The amount read by the student who is fluent in English depends on the ability of the ELL student.

- Provide programs for families of ELL students. Teach them how to check out books and obtain public library cards, and show them simple strategies for reading with their children (Gilliam, Gerla, & Wright, 2004).
- Record a variety of stories in English with a slow pace and clear English. Record small amounts of text so that students can listen several times and read back that portion of the story aloud.
- Send home specially recorded books and stories for extra practice (parents and siblings can use them as well).
- Show students how to sound out words in their native language, if it is orthographically phonetic. After sufficient experiences in their native language, have students apply this knowledge to English words with strong sound/symbol relationships.

PRINCIPLE #9: ACTIVE PARTICIPATION BY FAMILIES PROMOTES LITERACY

Within the past decade, the idea of "family as educator" has grown dramatically (Aurback, 1995; Benjamin & Lord, 1996; Neuman, Caperelli, & Kee, 1998). Families are a valuable resource for schools. They can use assisted reading methods and questioning techniques at home with their children. At school, they can help to create materials, listen to children read, and help to run book fairs.

Workshops can be offered at convenient times to help families understand the importance of reading at home, select books for their children, develop techniques for reading aloud, use recorded readings and hands-on materials, and so on.

Recommended Strategies

- Hold workshops regularly at convenient times. Provide snacks and time for socializing and bonding.
- Provide information about reading styles, especially the importance of accommodating students' perceptual strengths (visual, auditory, tactile, kinesthetic).
- Provide helpful reading information for families depending on their needs. Examples: lists of recommended children's books, procedures for securing library cards, creating good reading environments in the home, and suggestions for reading aloud to children.
- Teach family members a variety of assisted reading methods for increasing reading fluency and comprehension.
- Discuss and read excerpts from exemplary children's literature, and distribute lists of books.

- Demonstrate simple questioning strategies that family members can use to stimulate language and thinking.
- Have a "read in." These are often held in the evening. Family members, teachers, and the principal read to small groups of children. Create a relaxed atmosphere with some blankets, stuffed animals, and snacks.

PRINCIPLE #10: EVERY INDIVIDUAL HAS A SPECIAL LEARNING STYLE FOR READING, OR "READING STYLE"

Students learn with greater ease and enjoyment when they learn through their strengths and preferences, rather than through their weaknesses (Barber, Carbo, & Thomasson, 1998; Carbo 1997a, 1997b, 1998; Oglesby & Suter, 1995; Snyder, 1994, 1997). A student's reading style can be identified with observation techniques, assessment checklists, and a diagnostic questionnaire called the Reading Style Inventory® (RSI) (Carbo, 1992). The RSI identifies a youngster's reading style and recommends reading methods and materials compatible with a student's reading style. Many reading style instruments are displayed and discussed in Chapters 4 and 5, as well as Appendix E.

In general, primary children and at-risk readers tend to be strongly global, tactile, and kinesthetic (Atchinson & Brown, 1988; Duhaney & Ewing, 1998; Dunn, Griggs, Olson, Gorman, & Beasley, 1995; Mohrmann, 1990; Sudzina, 1993; Thies, 1999/2000; Wilson, 1993). For at-risk readers with this style, the pace of learning to read is sharply accelerated when holistic reading methods are used that include fun and movement, stories that students like and can choose, motivating role models, sufficient modeling of stories, and small amounts of skill work that are related to the stories, preferably in a game format.

Recommended Strategies

- Begin by accommodating students' reading styles with comfortable reading areas, healthy snacks, some areas with reduced lighting, and choices of activities.
- Use colored overlays to minimize dyslexia and other visual problems (see Chapter 10).
- Identify students' reading styles, especially those of your at-risk readers. Observe your students carefully. The checklists in Chapter 4 are helpful for doing this.
- Learn and use a variety of reading methods. Chapters 5–7 describe when and how to use many effective, research-based reading methods. If a reading method isn't working, use one that does.

- Many at-risk readers are global learners. This style responds well to stories and situations that are exciting, fun, adventurous, mysterious, humorous, and personal. Global students need to be highly interested in what they're reading to do their best.
- Global students need to be exposed to many high-quality authors and books. Here's a simple technique for creating interest in different authors. Select five to ten high-interest books or short stories. Read a very small portion of a story or book; then say "Who wants to read this one?" Hand it to a student who is interested. Then do the same with the next book or story, and so on.
- Use assisted reading methods, particularly the special recording technique described in Chapter 7, so that students are continually stretched to more difficult and more interesting reading material.
- Provide opportunities for movement and an informal reading area with rugs, pillows, and soft chairs. This will enable students to shift their reading/working positions often if they need mobility.
- Don't label students as "slow" just because they are primarily tactile and kinesthetic. Most young children are tactile and kinesthetic, or T-K. Tactile students learn well with hands-on materials, such as board games, bingo, and task cards; kinesthetic students learn through whole-body movement, including pantomime and floor games. Some students remain highly tactile and kinesthetic not just in the early grades but throughout their lives. Often these students are placed in lower tracks simply because their learning needs have not been met.

PRINCIPLE #11: MATCHING STUDENTS' READING STYLES MAKES LEARNING TO READ EASIER AND MORE ENJOYABLE

Every reading method, strategy, and set of materials is biased in favor of particular reading styles. Some students have many strengths and can learn with practically any reading approach. Others with some weaknesses need instruction that capitalizes on the learning strengths they do have. Most important, research indicates that matching students' reading styles, or learning strengths, is an important factor in increasing reading achievement and enjoyment (Barber, Carbo, & Thomasson, 1998; Brooks, 1991; Hodgin & Wooliscroft, 1997; LaShell, 1986; Oglesby & Suter, 1995; Skipper, 1997; Snyder, 1997).

Recommended Strategies

- When using basal readers, make necessary adaptations for those students who need them, especially those who are global, tactile, and kinesthetic. Try a human-interest story about the author or illustrator, have students pantomime or role-play a story, create vocabulary task cards, or tape-record the story.

- On occasion, give students the choice of working alone or in pairs on workbook pages. Let them read and discuss the directions and do the work together.
- Eliminate workbook pages and stories that students find confusing or boring. If a workbook page is important but confusing, try any of these three strategies: work with the students and guide them through the page; have students work together in pairs as you rotate from pair to pair and provide help; or create a game that practices the skill. Chapters 8 and 12 have more ideas on this topic.
- When possible, divide difficult tasks into small segments. Work on them for short periods, at the time of day when the energy of your students is high.
- Adapt and combine reading methods as needed. Many suggestions are in Chapter 6.

Figure 2.2   This young boy is pointing to the pictures and describing his reading style strengths and preferences to his classmates. As the photo shows, one of his preferences is to read with a friend.

PRINCIPLE # 12: STUDENTS WHO UNDERSTAND THEIR OWN READING STYLE LEARN TO WORK THROUGH THEIR STRENGTHS AND DEVELOP RESPECT FOR THE STYLES OF OTHERS

When youngsters understand that they have learning strengths and how they learn best, they are heartened, especially older students. As obvious as it may seem, tactile students don't always realize that writing down information a few times will help them to remember it, or that tracing over words will help them learn how to spell the words. Auditory students are often amazed at how quickly they learn to spell words if they record the words and their spellings ("talk, t-a-l-k, talk"), and then listen to the tape a few times in preparation for a test. And highly visual students can benefit from using flash cards to study their spelling words.

When students' natural strengths and preferences are accommodated, learning across content areas improves (Dunn et al., 1995; Snyder, 1997). Teach students that their reading style needs must not infringe on the needs of others. For example, if some students learn through discussion, they cannot confer near students who need quiet. Understanding and respecting diverse styles of learning provides continuing benefits to students throughout their lives.

Recommended Strategies

- Teach the concept of reading styles to students. For elementary students, read-aloud books that accentuate differences in styles, such as *Rose and Tulip* (Fels, 1993), or *Gregory the Terrible Eater* (Sharmat, 1980). For secondary students, *The Bedspread* (Fair, 1982) is a good choice.
- As appropriate, share reading styles information with your students, especially information about global/analytic styles and perceptual strengths.
- Create bulletin boards that highlight and describe students' different styles.
- Have students interview and compare the styles of their teachers, friends, and family.

Many students, especially older youngsters written off as unteachable, have made extremely high reading gains in short periods of time. Great teachers enable students to learn through their strengths and gain in self-confidence and motivation; then the false ceilings and barriers that hold them back can be greatly reduced or eliminated.

IN THE NEXT CHAPTER . . .

In Chapter 3, we'll look at the five reading areas and place the focus where it needs to be—on increasing reading comprehension (the goal of *all* reading instruction) and on reading for pleasure. We'll look at some of the shortest routes for accomplishing these two most important reading goals.

3

Focus on Comprehension and Enjoyment

There are many competing ideas about the best way to teach reading, but research places these two goals at the top of the list: First, we want our students to read and comprehend at high levels. Second, we want them to enjoy reading so that they read a great deal voluntarily.

Students who like to read and who read often for their own pleasure are likely to improve their reading skills at a much faster rate than students who don't (Allington, 2001; Anderson, 1996; Cipielewski & Stanovich, 1992; Krashen, 1993). Such students are called "engaged readers" in the literature. These are youngsters who take books out of the library and read for substantial amounts of time for their own enjoyment. As a teacher, you definitely want to do everything you can to help your students become highly engaged readers. Here's why: The amount of engaged reading is an excellent predictor of reading achievement. Apparently, the cognitive abilities required to perform well in reading comprehension (our most important goal), as well as reading fluency and vocabulary, are developed and strengthened through large amounts of engaged reading (Guthrie, Shafter, & Huang, 2001).

Before leaving this important topic, let's be clear that engaged reading is not assigned readings, nor is it affected by extrinsic rewards, such as distributing points or gifts. Engaged reading is reading that students do *because they want to read.*

Our most important reading goals, then, are to improve students' reading comprehension and to make the process of learning to read so enjoyable that all readers want to and do read a great deal for their own pleasure.

Great teachers of reading are very clear about these reading goals. Consequently, they accomplish high gains with their students. They eliminate (or use only minimally) reading strategies and materials that cause students great stress and/or reduce comprehension and reading for pleasure.

THE FIVE READING AREAS ARE NOT EQUAL

Currently, the No Child Left Behind Act tells us that we should teach and balance these five reading areas: phonemics, phonics, fluency, vocabulary, and comprehension.

The five reading areas are grouped together as if they are equal. But they are not equal! The first four reading areas all serve one purpose: to increase comprehension. *Comprehension is the goal of all reading instruction* (Greer, 2002). Phonemics and phonics instruction enables many children to decode unknown words, which can help them to read and better understand a story. Adequate fluency is important because slow, halting readers expend so much energy figuring out words that little energy is left for understanding *what* they are reading. Finally, a good vocabulary helps students to understand the meanings of words within a passage, giving them a better chance to fully understand the passage.

Research does point the way toward which reading procedures and strategies work best for most youngsters in the five areas and how we need to differentiate instruction to accommodate struggling readers.

Phonemics

Phonemics and phonics are not the same. Instruction in phonemics helps children to become aware of sounds *in spoken words,* whereas the teaching of phonics is meant to increase awareness of sounds *in written words.* Phonemics instruction is important. It helps to make children more aware of words and prepares them to learn phonics (Adams, 1990; Fischer & Carter, 1994; Hiebert, Pearson, Taylor, Richardson & Paris, 1998; National Reading Panel, 2000).

Good phonemics instruction

- precedes the teaching of phonics.
- is particularly appropriate for young children, like those in prekindergarten and kindergarten programs.
- is generally *playful,* taking only a few minutes daily for several weeks or months.

- is most effective with small groups of children.
- can include a variety of activities, such as rhyming words; identifying the number of words in a phrase or the number of syllables in a word; identifying initial, medial, and ending consonants; and taking apart words and putting them together (segmenting and blending).

Differentiated phonemics instruction

- varies in its goals and intensity depending on the readiness of the child and the youngster's reading style. Some young children, especially those who have auditory weaknesses, may be ready for only the simplest phonemics activities, such as rhyming words, identifying words that begin with the same sound, or counting the number of words in a phrase. Young, advanced readers and those with a strong global style may not require much, if any, phonemics instruction to become good readers.

Phonics

Before students are taught phonics, they should have a good idea of what reading actually *is*. Therefore, before phonics instruction begins, good teachers read a wide variety of printed materials to young children *at least* twice daily for 10 to 15 minutes, write down and share children's dictated stories, and read predictable books frequently. Predictable books are excellent for developing in children a sense of rhymes, word patterns, and story patterns—all of which help children to better understand what reading is (Bridge, Winograd, & Haley, 1983; Yopp, 1995).

Good phonics instruction

- makes up about one quarter of a total reading program in first grade. After studying 100,000 research experiments in reading, the National Research Council (NRC) recommended the following time allotments for a model first-grade two-hour language arts block: 30 minutes of writing, 30 minutes of free reading (trade books and stories), 30 minutes of structured or guided reading, and 30 minutes of skill development (activities such as spelling, phonics, word walls, and so on) (Manzo, 1998).
- can include the use of patterned texts that contain "repetitive vocabulary and language patterns" (p. 35, Strickland, 2007).
- is generally finished by the middle or end of second grade (Anderson, Hiebert, Wilkinson, & Scott, 1985; Stahl, 1992). An important exception to this recommendation is youngsters who are ready for only small amounts of simple phonics instruction in the early grades, or

those who did not receive effective phonics instruction in the early grades and who would benefit from it in later grades.

- focuses on words, *not* rules. Good readers decode new words by comparing them to patterns within words they already know (Adams, 1990). Good phonics teachers draw children's attention to word patterns rather than rules, and provide practice using texts that contain those same word patterns (Cunningham, 1991, 2000; Gaskins et al., 1988; Johnston, 1999).

- is direct and clear. Good phonics teachers are clear in their directions to children.

- enables children to identify new words quickly. The purpose of phonics instruction is not for children to laboriously sound out words. It is to enable youngsters to recognize words quickly so that they can focus on the *meaning* of what they are reading (Stahl, 1992; Stahl, Duffy-Hester & Stahl, 1998).

- may include invented spelling in the early grades. Research indicates that invented spelling improves children's writing and phonic awareness and does not appear to harm their reading or spelling (Clarke, 1989; Slavin, 1991).

Differentiated phonics instruction

- does not belabor the teaching of phonics for the following two groups: (a) advanced readers who may need only small amounts of phonics instruction to improve their spelling; and (b) students with severe auditory weaknesses who are capable of learning only small amounts of phonics. If students have great difficulty learning phonics, then large amounts of phonics are not appropriate and can cause unnecessary feelings of failure. For these students, teach small amounts of phonics as they are able to learn it. *Fit the program to the child, not the child to the program.*

- does not assume that a student has been adequately taught phonics in the lower grades. Phonics can be taught to any student at any age. Some struggling readers might have been poorly taught phonics, or they might not have been ready for phonics instruction when it was taught. If their auditory abilities matured late, they might make excellent candidates for phonics. Great teachers of reading constantly tune in to the needs, abilities, and strengths of their students.

Fluency

Fluent readers read rapidly, accurately, and with good expression. When children can read rapidly and accurately, the brain is freed to attend to the meaning of what is being read. The assisted reading methods in Chapters 6 and 7 are excellent for developing fluency.

Good fluency instruction

- provides many good, fluid models of reading (live or recorded).
- uses high-interest reading materials to aid retention.
- stresses comprehension, not speed. A reading pace that is too fast for a student can *reduce comprehension.*
- focuses on both automaticity (Perfetti, 1985; Stanovich, 1980) and prosody, or reading with expression (Dowhower, 1991).
- uses a variety of assisted reading methods, such as shared reading, neurological impress, echo reading, recorded readings, choral reading, and paired reading.
- increases students' fluency and comprehension with special, slow-paced recordings of challenging, high-interest reading material, recorded in small amounts. Students listen to a passage two or three times, and then read it aloud (Carbo, 1978a, 1978b, 1989, 1992).
- encourages nonfluid readers to listen to brief, fluid reading models and then to practice reading aloud the modeled passage repeatedly until they can read it fluidly, before reading the passage aloud to others (Samuels, 1988).
- does not require struggling readers to read aloud unless they have practiced a passage and are ready to read aloud.
- monitors and assists nonfluent readers often as they read aloud to their peers and to their teacher.
- does not take frequent word counts. This practice can reduce students' comprehension and reading for pleasure. A discussion of word counts may be found toward the end of Chapter 7.

Differentiated fluency instruction

- provides the specific assisted reading methods that will assure success for each struggling reader.
- uses high-level, challenging reading materials with struggling readers (Carbo, 1978a; Chomsky, 1978; Heckelman, 1969).
- asks struggling readers to read back passages they have practiced in a variety of ways, depending on the confidence of the reader. For example, those with little confidence might choral-read their passage back with a teacher, buddy, or a group.
- provides a variety of high-interest, reading materials recorded so that the printed words and spoken words are synchronized for students.

Figure 3.1   Extensive reading builds reading fluency and enables students to read and recall a large number of sight words and their meanings.

SOURCE: Printed with permission from the National Reading Styles Institute, Syosset, NY.

Vocabulary

Oral and reading vocabularies differ. Oral vocabulary refers to words that we understand when we hear them and words that we use when we speak. Reading vocabulary refers to printed words that we understand as we read. Most students—indeed, all of us—have different oral and reading vocabularies. Our reading vocabulary is generally much larger. Students with large reading vocabularies have a better chance of comprehending what they read. Most important, children learn most of their words in indirect ways, such as listening to adults and other children speak, being read to, conversing, and reading on their own (Greer, 2002).

Research strongly indicates that extensive reading enables students to read and recall a large number of sight words and their meanings (Nagy, Anderson, & Herman, 1987; Nagy, Herman, & Anderson, 1985; Stahl, 1999; Stanovich, 2000; Sternberg, 1987; Swanborn & de Glopper, 1999). In fact, beginning about third grade, the amount of reading done by students is the "major determinant of vocabulary growth" (Nagy & Anderson, 1984, p. 327). Reading words in context helps to build a sight vocabulary and increases the reader's knowledge of word meanings.

Good vocabulary instruction

- provides animated readings of materials that stretch students so that they become increasingly familiar with a variety of high-level words in the context of high-interest stories.
- uses the Continuum of Assisted Reading Methods (see Chapter 6) to provide the modeling and repetition that enables students to read increasingly higher-level reading materials.
- engages children in discussions about words.
- uses videos, visuals, and anecdotes to expand word meaning.
- provides strategies for deciphering unknown words, including the study of prefixes, suffixes, and roots.
- teaches children when and how to use dictionaries and reference aids. Note: Dictionary definitions do not work well for many students (McKeown, 1993; Miller & Gildea, 1987; Nagy & Scott, 2000).

Differentiated vocabulary instruction

- uses recorded stories and books that engage students and stretch their abilities. In this way, vocabulary is introduced within a high-interest context.
- uses many hands-on vocabulary games, especially for tactile learners.
- schedules weekly challenges to encourage students to expand their vocabulary.
- provides word meanings for struggling readers as they read so as not to interrupt the flow of the story.
- provides an overview and key words in a story, in the primary language of English language learners.

Comprehension

Finally, we arrive at the ultimate goal of all reading instruction: text comprehension (Greer, 2002). Good readers are purposeful readers; their brains are always working and thinking while they read (Anderson, Hiebert, Wilkinson, & Scott, 1985).

Good comprehension instruction

- sets the mood of a story and provides opportunities for dramatizations, such as readers' theater, puppetry, and role playing.
- helps children to monitor their comprehension by asking key questions and, at times, modeling the thinking process while reading a story.
- uses graphic and semantic organizers (organizational pictures of the text content).

Figure 3.2   Before beginning a new class topic, the students put up individual Post-its indicating what they know (under the "K"), and what they want to know (under the "W"). At the end of their study, they write what they have learned about the topic under the "L."

SOURCE: Photo courtesy of O'Connor Elementary School, Victoria, TX.

- asks questions about what children have read, especially questions that require higher-level skills, such as drawing conclusions, making inferences, and predicting.
- teaches children to generate and ask their own reading questions; also, encourages the use of different colored markers so that students can highlight in the same color a comprehension question and the sentence or sentences within a passage that provide the answer.
- makes children aware of story structure (Pearson & Camperell, 1994).

- provides hands-on games that practice comprehension skills, including summarizing, predicting, cause and effect, categorizing, comparing and contrasting.
- provides many choices of nonfiction and fiction reading materials on topics of great interest to students, especially boys (Duke, 2000; Lange, 1986; Pappas, 1993). For older students, classroom libraries need to include stories about sports, animals, cars, trucks, scary events, and popular culture, as well as series books, funny books, magazines, comics, and cartoons (Moorman & Turner, 1999).

Differentiated comprehension instruction

- provides an overview of a story in the primary language of English language learners so that these students are better able to understand the English version of the story.
- provides recordings of stories dictated by a struggling reader so that the youngster can learn to read his or her own story. This strategy is especially helpful for older students reading at very low reading levels. The student's dictated stories should be very brief, about three to seven sentences. As soon as possible, transition the student to stories and books written by other authors.
- allows students to partner and discuss comprehension questions before responding to the questions on a worksheet or a test.

STAY FOCUSED ON COMPREHENSION AND ENJOYMENT

Keep in mind that the simple goal of *all* reading instruction—including instruction in phonemics, phonics, fluency, and vocabulary—is to improve reading comprehension and to make learning to read enjoyable. If a reading program confuses or bores students, then it's doing more harm than good. If possible, it should be changed or discarded. As discussed previously, many of today's reading programs teach far too many minuscule reading skills, use too many worksheets, are scripted and unresponsive to students' needs, and don't provide reading materials that students prefer, especially boys. The result? Only one-third of our students are reading at or above grade level, and reading for pleasure declines every year. Those figures have remained the same for well over a decade.

By focusing your energies where they should be—on reading comprehension and enjoyment—you are more likely to make learning to read easy and nurture a love of reading in all your students. Reading for pleasure helps to increase reading ability, so give your students the gift that keeps on giving: Make your reading program fun!

Figure 3.3   Engaged readers enjoy reading, and they read a great deal. Large amounts of voluntary reading improve reading fluency, vocabulary, and comprehension.

SOURCE: Photo courtesy of Bob Hope Elementary School, San Antonio, TX.

IN THE NEXT CHAPTER . . .

I'll discuss the importance of identifying students' reading styles with observation techniques and checklists, and then teaching them through their strengths and preferences. Chapters 4 and 5 are at the heart of differentiating instruction and becoming a great teacher of reading.

4

Identify Natural Strengths

In this chapter, we'll look at what reading styles are, why they're important, and how to identify them. Place two children of similar back-
grounds and intelligence in the same reading class. Both are attentive and
well-behaved; both want to learn to read. The teacher follows exactly the
Teacher's Guide for whatever reading program is being used. One child
learns to read easily; the other does not. Why? It's highly probable that,
working quite by chance, the teacher matched the reading style of the successful reader and mismatched the reading style of the child who did not
learn to read easily.

But learning to read should *not* be a gamble. By placing the focus
where it needs to be—on the individual student—great teachers of reading
effectively differentiate instruction and improve the odds for all students.

WHAT ARE READING STYLES?

Everyone has a special learning style for reading, or "reading style." You
have one, and so does each of your students. Reading styles describes a
person's learning strengths and preferences *during the act of reading.* The
study of reading styles considers how a student's ability to learn to read
is affected by the reader's (1) immediate environment, (2) emotional
makeup, (3) sociological preferences, (4) physical needs, and (5) style of
processing information. My work in reading styles is based on the model

of learning styles developed by Rita and Kenneth Dunn. Researchers and practitioners throughout the United States have reported significantly improved student attitudes and higher achievement after implementing practices based on the Dunn and Dunn Model of Learning Styles (Alberg, et al., 1992; Cain, & Norwood, 2000; DeBello, 1990; Dunn, & Dunn, 1999; Dunn, et al., 1995; Dunn, & Griggs, 2003–2004; Tendy, & Geisert, 1998). For more information see www.learning styles.net.

Figure 4.1   This chart of the Dunn and Dunn Model of Learning Styles helps students understand how they learn best.

SOURCE: Photo by Linda Queiruga. Courtesy of Canyon del Oro High School, Tucson, AZ.

Each of us—not just students labeled "at risk" or "disabled"—has varying learning strengths and weaknesses. Not only does every person have a distinctly different reading style, but every reading method, resource, and teaching strategy demands particular reading style strengths of the learner. Your reading style determines how well you concentrate and read with particular reading methods, materials, and activities, and under certain conditions. Research tells us that matching students' reading styles makes learning to read easier, increases student motivation, and improves achievement, with some at-risk readers making reading gains 10 times greater than their previous progress (Acceleration Program, 1998; Barber, Carbo, & Thomasson, 1998; Bradsby, Wise, Mundell, & Haas, 1992;

Brooks, 1991; Catalog of School Reform Models, 1998, 2002, 2006; Hodgin & Wooliscroft, 1997; LaShell, 1986; Oglesby & Suter, 1995; Skipper, 1997; Snyder, 1997).

READING STYLE OF AT-RISK READERS

An important key to differentiating instruction for at-risk readers is to know that, as a group, they tend to be global, tactile, kinesthetic learners (Duhaney & Ewing, 1998; Dunn, Griggs, Olson, Gorman, & Beasley, 1995; Mohrmann, 1990; Sudzina, 1993; Wilson, 1993). They also tend to have a high need for mobility, intake (food and drink), soft lighting, opportunities to work with their peers, and they prefer to read during the late morning. Often these students dislike reading due to strong feelings of boredom and failure. Those behaviors can change dramatically when they are given reading materials of their choice and the reading methods that enable them to read those materials.

Given the fact that less than one-third of our students read at or above their grade level (Bracey, 2006), it's clear that our students need effective, differentiated reading instruction. Business as usual—the traditional teacher-directed classroom with its lectures, board work, and worksheets—has not worked for our students, especially those in the bottom third academically. Many of these youngsters are not only *mistaught* with primarily analytic approaches, they are also *mistested* with skills exercises designed for analytics.

Too often, when our students fail, they are blamed, retained, and placed in special education classes. Many of these students are poor, minority, and immigrant children who cannot function even at the most basic level of literacy. During the past two decades, however, teaching grounded in the reading styles model has demonstrated the power to bring about rapid results with these youngsters (see Appendix C).

Teaching grounded in reading styles focuses reading instruction where it should be: on students' strengths and preferences. For example, teachers who use a standard basal program make many adaptations for their students. They read high-interest stories aloud frequently to their students, reduce the number of worksheets, allow students to work in pairs, skip stories that students find boring, reduce the amount of phonics for students with low auditory abilities, and supplement their program with high-interest, recorded short stories, assisted reading methods, and hands-on games that help the children master important reading skills quickly.

In other words, the students' reading styles *drive the instruction*—not an outside system of teaching or a set of commercial materials. This paradigm shift is *critical*. We are losing millions of students trying to fit them into systems that actually prevent them from learning. Although some students have been able to adapt, the low reading abilities of the great majority of our students offer ample testimony that many cannot.

MATCHING READING STYLES: THREE IMPORTANT RESEARCH FINDINGS

Three research findings are worth noting here:

- Matching students' reading styles has brought about improvement in reading achievement and enjoyment in short periods of time.
- Today's emphasis on worksheets, lecture, rigid structure, and extensive skill instruction is particularly counterproductive for at-risk students—especially boys.
- Instructional practices that overemphasize testing, long periods of sitting, and provide few or no choices of reading materials seriously mismatch the reading styles of many students, especially at-risk readers who tend to be global, tactile, and kinesthetic.

Flippo (1998) reported that reading experts placed the following reading practices among those that made learning to read *difficult* for students: the use of too many worksheets, boring stories, skills taught in isolation, a focus on skill instruction instead of comprehension, few or no choices of reading materials, and following teacher editions faithfully instead of responding to the needs of students (see Chapter 2).

IDENTIFYING STUDENTS' READING STYLES

Let's look at two ways to identify students' reading styles: observing the students, and the use of checklists. In Chapter 6, we'll work with the Reading Style Inventory and ways of matching students' reading styles with appropriate reading methods and materials.

We begin with a simple way to identify reading styles: by watching the behavior of students! When a student chooses to do something in the same way, repeatedly, those choices often provide an indication of the youngster's preferred style. For example, students who can recall what they hear very well, who understand verbal directions easily, and who like read-aloud stories are displaying the characteristics of auditory learners. Those who shift in their seats often and cannot sit still for long periods, who are restless and must move about, may be kinesthetic learners who need greater mobility.

Since students tend to select activities that match their reading styles, you can begin to identify your students' reading styles by providing them with acceptable choices. For students unaccustomed to making choices, provide just two clear choices at first. As students become more adept, increase the number of choices. Here are three procedures you may wish to try:

1. To identify perceptual strengths: "Describe your favorite scene in this story. You may draw or write about it (visual/tactile), pantomime it (kinesthetic), or discuss it (auditory)."

Figure 4.2   Reading Style Observation Guide

Observation	Reading Style Diagnosis	Suggested Strategies for Teaching Reading
The student:	**The student:**	
1. Is distracted by noise, looks up from reading at the slightest sound, places hands over ears, tries to quiet others.	Prefers to read in a quiet environment.	⇨ Provide quiet reading areas such as study carrels and carpeted sections; use rugs, stuffed furniture, drapes to absorb sound; make available headsets to block noise.
2. Squirms, fidgets, squints when reading near a window on a sunny day.	Prefers to read in soft or dim light.	⇨ Use plants, curtains, hanging beads, dividers to block and diffuse light; add shaded lamps to reading areas.
3. Enjoys reading with the teacher.	Prefers reading with adults.	⇨ Schedule youngster to read with you often; try using older tutors.
4. Cannot complete lengthy assignments.	May not be persistent or responsible.	⇨ Give short reading assignments and check them frequently; try short stories.
5. Becomes confused by many choices of reading materials.	Requires structure.	⇨ Limit choices; give clear, simple directions; try a structured reading approach.
6. Enjoys choices, demonstrates creativity when reading.	Does not require structure.	⇨ Provide many choices of reading materials; give many options for project work.
7. Participates actively in group discussions; chooses to read with friends.	Prefers to read with peers.	⇨ Establish areas where small groups can read together; provide reading games, activities.
8. Notices and remembers details in pictures; is a good speller; does not confuse visually similar words ("stop" and "spot").	Is a visual learner.	⇨ Try a whole-word reading approach; picture-word games; puzzels, graphs, diagrams.
9. Remembers directions and stories after hearing them;decodes words with ease; enjoys listening activities.	Is an auditory learner.	⇨ Try a phonic or linguistic reading approach; use listening activities.
10. Enjoys learning by touching; remembers words after tracing over and "feeling" them; likes to type, play reading games; is very active.	Is a tactile/kinesthetic learner.	⇨ Try a language-experience approach; use clay, sandpaper, to form words; try many reading games, model building, project work, multisensory resources.

SOURCE: © Marie Carbo, 1984.

2. To identify sociological preferences: "You may do this activity alone, with a partner, or with a small group."

3. To identify environmental preferences: "You may do this activity at your desk, on the rug, or at one of the tables."

Figure 4.2 provides 10 teacher observations, interprets those observations, and recommends appropriate instructional strategies and materials.

IDENTIFYING GLOBAL AND ANALYTIC STYLES

1. *Teacher Observations.* One of the most interesting lists describing the differences between global and analytic children was provided by teachers (Figure 4.3). In comparing the two styles, teachers described their global students as youngsters who enjoy life, like projects and games, are creative with their toys, have a "do it tomorrow" philosophy, and are often messy, social, and flexible. When describing their analytic students, teachers said that they are first to get their books out and to pick up and straighten, have neat clothes closets, play by the rules, and like schedules (these students remind teachers when it's time for certain subjects).

2. *Global/Analytic Checklist.* Another technique for identifying global and analytic styles is the Global/Analytic Checklist in Figure 4.4. This list tells us that strong analytics can piece together details to form a whole; they tend to be list makers, good planners, logical, organized, punctual, tidy, and so on. Strongly global people need to understand the "big picture" to draw their interest to a subject. They tend to be emotional, intuitive, spontaneous, and creative. They often like to learn with anecdotes and humor, and they like to do many things at once. You're likely to find that many students are not extremely global or analytic. Instead, they may be a combination of both styles (Burke et al., 1999–2000). As a group, however, young children and at-risk readers, tend to be more strongly global than analytic.

DIFFERENTIATED STRATEGIES FOR GLOBALS AND ANALYTICS

Figure 4.5 suggests strategies for teaching globals and analytics. These strategies are helpful for understanding the frustrations of students who are extremely global or extremely analytic. For example, charts with rules (analytic item #2) are helpful for analytics, but for globals an explanation of *why* the rules are needed, along with positive feedback when rules are followed, will usually work better. And although global children do like to hear many stories (including interesting personal stories from the teacher),

Figure 4.3   Teachers' descriptions of strongly global vs. strongly analytic children.

Global	Analytic
• Enjoy life	• Play by the rules
• Creative with toys	• Line things up
• Do-it-tomorrow philosophy	• Desks are very tidy
• "Messy"	• Know where things are
• Keep what they need around them	• Correct people
• If it's in a pile it exists; otherwise, it's forgotten	• Don't like changes
• Can't find things	• Can verbalize assignments
• Social	• Like to stay on schedule
• Go with the flow	• First to get books out
• Flexible	• Clothes closets neat
• Can see many answers	• Pick up and straighten

analytics generally have a lower tolerance for anything that draws the class away from a learning task for what they consider too long a period of time. Considering that most classes have students who are strongly global, strongly analytic, and everything in between, it's certainly not easy to satisfy the needs of all learners. But remember, the majority of at-risk readers tend to have strong global tendencies.

Let's look at the strategies for globals and analytics in another way. The strategies in Figure 4.5 are not meant to be rigidly applied, because students' reading styles are complex. For example, Strategies 1–3 on the "Global" list are beneficial for both analytics and globals. Brain research tells us that providing overviews, an emotional link to the learner, and connecting a reading program to the real world are generally beneficial for all types of learners. It's also true that some global youngsters do not follow the typical pattern for global learners; these students may be strongly global but not strongly tactile and kinesthetic, and they may not learn best with a great deal of movement. Thus for these particular global students, Strategies 5, 9, and 10 might be inappropriate. Always be aware of each student's basic learning needs and choose the strategies that are most appropriate for a particular youngster.

Global students respond to reading materials that involve them emotionally. *Sight Words That Stick* (Figure 4.6) uses humorous, exciting stories and pictures to indelibly imprint sight words on the minds of students. A similar technique is used for older students with *Vocabulary Cartoons* (Figure 4.7). The unusual rhyming associations are particularly beneficial for older global students in helping them recall the words and their meanings.

Figure 4.4   Are You Global? Analytic? Or Both?

To help you determine whether you are predominantly global or analytic or a mixture of both styles, take the Global/Analytic Reading Styles Checklist. Parents or teachers may want to complete this checklist for children who are too young to do it themselves.

Global/Analytic Reading Styles Checklist

Scoring Key:

Strongly Analytic 9-10	Strongly Global 9-10
Moderately Analytic 6-8	Moderately Global 6-8
Somewhat Analytic 3-5	Somewhat Global 3-5
Slightly Analytic 0-2	Slightly Global 0-2

Analytic People Often:

_____ Recall what they hear

_____ Make decisions based on logic

_____ Recall facts and names

_____ Are good planners

_____ Like to work in a highly organized environment

_____ Are very punctual

_____ Like to do one thing at a time

_____ Are meticulous about their work

_____ Learn when information is presented sequentially, step-by-step

_____ Speak with few gestures

My Analytic Score_____

Global People Often:

_____ Recall what they see, touch, feel

_____ Make decisions based on their emotions and intuition

_____ Recall visual images and faces

_____ Are spontaneous

_____ Like to work in a less organized environment

_____ May not be punctual—unless the event is very important

_____ Like to do many things at once

_____ Like to be creative

_____ Learn when information is presented in a story, especially with humor

_____ Speak with many gestures

My Global Score_____

Scoring Directions: Add the number of checked items for each column and determine your score from the Scoring Key at the top of the page.

SOURCE: © Marie Carbo, 1990.

Figure 4.5   Differentiated Strategies for Globals and Analytics

---

Strategies for Teaching Globals

1. Begin lessons with overviews, jokes, anecdotes, drama.

2. Provide an emotional link to the learner with stories, jokes, personal experiences.

3. Connect your reading program to the real world. Use articles, interviews, magazines, television programs, news events.

4. Begin with the "big picture" of a story. Use overviews, visuals, videos. Then discuss details.

5. Include many tactile and kinesthetic experiences, such as games, trips, lab experiments, rocking chairs, painting.

6. Provide imaginative reading areas, such as cardboard castles, fireplaces, tents. Use soft light.

7. Use lots of color and humor. Make a colorful bulletin board of jokes and riddles.

8. Teach facts and concepts in story form. Be imaginative. Globals remember stories.

9. Provide breaks, short assignments. Check assignments often.

10. Use learning centers and games. Allow mobility.

11. Ask students for suggestions. Globals enjoy being creative!

Strategies for Teaching Analytics

1. State class rules and then follow them. Consistency is important.

2. List specific rules for projects and assignments. Analytics tend to function better with directions.

3. Outline procedures for grading. Bonus points, technical appraisals, and penalties need to be clear.

4. Give feedback on tests as quickly and completely as possible.

5. Provide sequential lessons. Processing of information is accomplished through a step-by-step activity.

6. Remember that details are important. Specifics that mention small, seemingly insignificant portions of information are often interesting to analytics.

7. Stay on topic. Too many personal experiences and random information tend to disturb analytics.

8. Itemize and summarize. These techniques provide structure to the lesson.

9. Provide key words or brief notes on the chalkboard or overhead transparency.

10. Follow the class schedule. Routine creates a predictable environment.

SOURCE: © Marie Carbo, 1990.

Figure 4.6   *Sight Words That Stick®* by Janet Martin

help

1) Patti (p) loved the ocean. She loved to swim in the water. One day Patti was swimming and having a great time.

2) Then Patti heard something. DUN, dun, dun, dun... DUN, dun, dun, dun... (sound from the movie *Jaws*)

    She saw a shark coming toward her! She held up her hand as high as she could and yelled, "**Help**!!! **Help**!!!"

SOURCE: Courtesy of the National Reading Styles Institute.

Figure 4.7   Vocabulary Cartoons by Sam, Max, and Bryan Burchers

CATAMARAN
(CAT uh muh ran)
a boat with two parallel hulls; a
raft of logs tied together

Sounds like: **CAT**

"A CAT CATAMARAN."

SOURCE: © Sam Burchers, 1998. Reprinted with permission from New Monic Books, Inc. www.vocabularycartoons.com.

IDENTIFYING MODALITY STRENGTHS

All of us—adults and children alike—take in information through our different senses: auditory, visual, tactile, and kinesthetic (see Figure 4.8).

Figure 4.8   Identifying Modality Strengths

Auditory Learners
- Detect differences in sounds among letters and words
- Recall what they hear
- Learn by listening and speaking

Visual Learners
- Detect visual differences among letters and words
- Recall what they see
- Learn by observing

Tactile Learners
- Detect differences in shapes and textures that they touch
- Recall what they touch
- Learn by writing, tracing, playing games

Kinesthetic Learners
- Detect differences in experiences
- Recall body movements, experiences, feelings
- Learn by performing and by most kinds of physical activity

SOURCE: © National Reading Styles Institute, 1996.

About 20% of our students can recall what they hear, while 40% are more likely to recall what they see. Many need to write or use manipulatives to recall facts easily. And some learn best with real-life activities, such as planning and running a book sale. An excellent technique for accommodating modality strengths is to provide alternative ways for students to demonstrate what they have learned.

Auditory Learners: Students Who Learn Easily by Listening

Watch a group during a lecture. Those who rarely write anything down are usually strongly auditory learners. They don't need to take notes because they can recall what they hear. Often writing down notes, they say, just interferes with listening and recalling. Auditory learners are able to learn through lecture and discussion, and they usually enjoy these activities. If they are *strongly* auditory, then visuals and hands-on materials may not be necessary. Such students are in the minority. In fact, few of our students find it easy to recall what they hear. That's especially true for at-risk students, who seldom are strongly auditory.

Auditory learners remember what they hear so well that they often can re-create what they heard. They store auditory information in their brains like a recording. In fact, recording and listening to information is an excellent way for these students to study for a test. Students who learn well by listening are at a great advantage in the traditional classroom, where lecture is used frequently. But auditory students are in the minority, so teachers who lecture frequently should provide visuals and breaks along the way, such as writing key words on the board, and showing slides, videos, and pictures that relate to the lecture. Another technique is to stop a lecture and have the students divide into small groups or pairs so that they can discuss what they've learned, answer a few questions about the lecture, or draw and caption a picture about what they've learned and share it with their partner.

Visual Learners: Students Who Learn Easily by Watching and Observing

Visual learners recall in detail what they see. They enjoy looking at pictures, and they learn easily with flash cards and reading through their notes. These students will take notes during a lecture not necessarily for the tactile feel of taking the notes, but so that they can create a visual representation of what they are hearing. Among their notes, they may add drawings, color, circle important concepts, make certain words larger, add large exclamation points—anything that makes the most important information stand out visually.

Tactile Learners: Students Who Learn Easily by Touching and Manipulating

Tactile learners like to use their hands while they are concentrating or learning. They remember what they write and may doodle, draw, crochet, or move their fingers during a lecture because the tactile movement helps them to remember what they are hearing and seeing. Often tactile learners do creative things well with their hands: sewing, baking, designing, painting, and crafts. Many young children and at-risk readers are strongly tactile learners.

For the most part, teachers rarely present new information in a tactile format. Tactile learners who are not auditory are at a disadvantage in a traditional classroom in which lecture is used a great deal. Auditory students need only listen in order to learn. Visual children can review their notes at home. Tactile students are not any less able, but they simply are seldom taught in the way they learn best. My colleagues and I have found that many tactile students benefit from the use of assisted reading methods and recorded readings, followed by skills taught with hands-on games.

Figure 4.9   Hanging words are ideal for the visual learner. Students are surrounded by words they are learning. Notice how the shape of the words is outlined for greater visual impact.

SOURCE: Photo courtesy of O'Connor Elementary School, Victoria, TX.

Figure 4.10   This highly tactile student is matching task cards that practice antonyms. See Chapter 8 for samples of task cards.

SOURCE: Photo courtesy of Jim Hill Middle School, Minot, ND.

Kinesthetic Learners: Students Who Learn Easily by Doing and Experiencing

Young children and at-risk readers often are kinesthetic learners. They may be students whose perceptual strengths mature more slowly than average, or they may be strongly kinesthetic all their lives. Kinesthetic learners are helped with frequent breaks that allow them movement, informal reading areas that enable them to stretch and move while they read, and projects or games that involve large muscles. They tend to like stories with lots of pictures and action, excitement, surprise, adventure, mystery, monsters, science fiction, and so on.

Kinesthetic students learn more easily when they are "doing" or building something related to what they're learning. They might act out or pantomime a story or words, build a scene from a story, create a reading game, interview a visiting author, and so on.

Figure 4.11   This highly kinesthetic student reads better when she rocks back and forth.

SOURCE: Courtesy of Howard Elementary School, Medford, OR.

Figure 4.12   Reading Styles Checklist for Identifying Perceptual Strengths

---

Identifying Auditory Strengths

12-14 = Excellent

9-11 = Good

5-8 = Moderate

0-4 = Poor to Fair

The student can:

___1. follow brief verbal instructions

___2. repeat simple sentences of 8 to 12 words

___3. remember a phone number after hearing it a few times

___4. recall simple math facts or a few lines of poetry after hearing them several times

___5. understand long sentences

___6. remember and be able to place in sequence events discussed

___7. use appropriate vocabulary and sentence structure

___8. pay attention to a story or lecture for 15 to 30 minutes

___9. concentrate on an auditory task even when an auditory distraction is presented

___10. identify and recall the sounds of individual letters

___11. discriminate between/among words that sound alike (e.g.,"leaf" and "leave" or "cot" and "cat")

___12. discriminate between/among letters that sound alike (e.g., "sh" and "ch" or "a" and "o")

___13. blend letters quickly to form words

___14. sound out words and still retain the storyline

SOURCE: © National Reading Styles Institute, 1986.

Figure 4.13   Identifying Visual Strengths

11-14 = Excellent

8-10 = Good

5-7 = Moderate

0-4 = Poor to Fair

The student can:

____1. follow simple instructions that are written and/or drawn

____2. place four to six pictures in proper story sequence

____3. recall a phone number after seeing it a few times

____4. concentrate on a visual activity for 15 to 30 minutes

____5. concentrate on a visual task when a visual distraction is presented

____6. work on a visual task without looking away or rubbing his or her eyes

____7. recall words after seeing them a few times

____8. remember and understand words accompanied by a pictorial representation

____9. read words without confusing the order of the letters (e.g., reading "spot" for "stop")

____10. discriminate between/among letters that look alike (e.g., "m" and "n" or "c," "e," and "o")

____11. discriminate between/among words that look alike (e.g., "fill" and "full" or "that" and "what")

____12. discriminate between/among letters and/or words that are mirror images (e.g., "b" and "d" or "saw" and "was")

____13. spell words easily that do not have a direct sound-symbol correspondence and must be recalled visually (e.g., "straight," "glue," "knuckle")

____14. read small print and understand drawings with intersecting lines, such as graphs, maps, or musical notes on a staff

SOURCE: © National Reading Styles Institute, 1986.

Figure 4.14   Identifying Tactile Strengths

11-13 = Excellent

8-10 = Good

5-7 = Moderate

0-4 = Poor to Fair

The student can:

_____1. draw and color pictures

_____2. perform crafts such as sewing, weaving, and/or making models

_____3. remember a phone number after dialing it a few times

_____4. concentrate on a tactile task for 15 to 30 minutes

_____5. hold a pen or pencil correctly

_____6. write legible letters of the alphabet appropriate in size for his or her age

_____7. write with correct spacing

_____8. recall words more easily after tracing over clay or sandpaper letters that form the words

_____9. remember words more easily after writing them a few times

_____10. recall words more easily after playing a game containing those words, such as bingo or dominoes

_____11. recall the names of objects more easily after touching them a few times

_____12. write words correctly more often after tracing over them with his or her finger

_____13. recall words more easily after typing them a few times

SOURCE: © National Reading Styles Institute, 1986.

Figure 4.15   Identifying Kinesthetic Strengths

10-12 = Excellent

  7-9 = Good

  4-6 = Moderate

  0-3 = Poor to Fair

The student can:

____1. run, walk, catch a ball, and so on, in a rhythmical, smooth fashion

____2. concentrate for 15 to 30 minutes during kinesthetic activities that require whole-body movement

____3. recall dances, games, sports, and/or directions after performing them a few times

____4. move his or her body easily and freely when acting in a play

____5. remember words seen on posters and signs when on a trip

____6. memorize a script more easily when actually performing in a play

____7. understand concepts after "experiencing" them in some way (e.g., going on a trip, acting in a play, caring for pets, performing experiments, and so on)

____8. remember words after "experiencing" them (e.g., looking at the word "apple" while eating an apple or pretending to be an elephant while learning the word "elephant")

____9. recall words used in a floor game more easily after playing the game a few times

____10. remember facts, poetry, lines in a play more easily when he or she is walking or running, rather than standing still

____11. recall a letter of the alphabet more easily after forming it with his or her entire body

____12. remember the "feeling" of a story better than the details

SOURCE: © National Reading Styles Institute, 1986.

GETTING STARTED

Here are 10 beginning recommendations for identifying and matching your students' reading style strengths:

1. Encourage awareness of different styles. You might start by having your students discuss or draw pictures of where they like to read and with whom.

2. Use the checklists and observation guides in this chapter to identify your students' global/analytic tendencies and perceptual strengths.

3. Use the Reading Style Inventory for a full analysis of your students' reading styles and matching strategies (see the end of Chapter 6 and Appendix E).

4. Begin lessons globally with anecdotes and visual aids that develop relevant concepts.

5. Provide adequate structure and some step-by-step skill work, especially for analytic learners.

6. Give students alternatives to written reports, such as pantomime, dioramas, dressing up as a book character, creating book jackets, or making a mobile.

7. Don't require students to do a report for each book they read (consider using the alternatives to written reports described above). Such practices can destroy a student's desire to read.

8. Have older students create reading games for younger ones. Use games instead of worksheets often, especially with at-risk readers.

9. Create small informal reading areas with rugs, pillows, and comfortable chairs.

10. Allow students to read alone or in pairs. Provide this choice at least some of the time.

DIFFERENTIATING INSTRUCTION FOR AT-RISK READERS

Differentiated instruction is most powerful when students' strengths and interests are both identified and accommodated, especially their global/analytic styles and perceptual strengths. In this chapter, we've looked at the most typical reading styles of young children and of at-risk readers (global, tactile, kinesthetic), along with differentiated strategies that accommodate different styles of learning. Unfortunately, many students become at-risk readers because of reading programs that teach them through their weaknesses and block their learning abilities. Their failures are absolutely unnecessary and can be remedied through teaching to their strengths. Strength teaching is the most powerful kind of teaching. Great teachers of reading are aware of and use this power.

IN THE NEXT CHAPTER . . .

We'll look at how great teachers of reading teach to the natural strengths of their students. We'll study the global and analytic models of teaching reading, match reading methods to students' strengths, and learn how to use the Reading Style Inventory® (RSI).

5

Teach to Natural Strengths

It's no surprise that many at-risk readers are global, tactile, and kinesthetic learners, for that is the reading style that is least accommodated in U.S. classrooms. Many of today's at-risk readers are dropouts of overly rigid reading programs, which match a strongly analytic/auditory reading style. Others fail because of too little or poor teaching, or the use of holistic reading approaches that provide insufficient modeling of text and too few decoding skills. It's important for teachers to know their students and teach to their natural strengths and interests.

THE NEED FOR DIFFERENTIATED READING INSTRUCTION

The International Reading Association provides this wise counsel in their excellent book *Making a Difference Means Making It Different: Honoring Children's Rights to Excellent Reading Instruction* (2000):

> Because children learn differently, teachers must be familiar with a wide range of proven methods for helping children gain these skills. They also must have thorough knowledge of the children they teach, so they can provide the appropriate balance of methods needed for each child. (p. 3)

Great teachers of reading know and understand their students' reading styles; they use this information, along with their own observations, to provide "the appropriate balance of methods needed for each child," especially for at-risk readers. When a reading method makes learning to read difficult for a youngster, it should be minimized or discarded. Reading methods should be used that make the most of a student's strengths and interests, and make the process of learning to read feel easy and pleasurable.

TEACH TO STUDENTS' NATURAL STRENGTHS

Every reading method demands specific reading style strengths and preferences of learners. Students' reading styles are so varied that no single reading approach can be effective for all learners. The reading methods used most often with students should accommodate their natural strengths.

For example, children with excellent auditory abilities respond well to phonic and linguistic approaches. Visual students learn well with methods that emphasize whole words or sentences. And language-experience approaches are appropriate for tactile youngsters who learn by writing, touching, and tracing over words (see Figure 5.1).

Some students with many modality strengths can learn to read with a wide variety of reading methods. But for students with few modality strengths, reading problems can develop quickly when the deficit model is used and these children are taught to read primarily through their weakest modalities. Strength teaching is powerful teaching. It helps to make learning to read easy and fun, and has resulted in high reading gains and reduced discipline problems (see Appendices C and D).

PROBLEMS CAUSED BY THE
DEFICIT MODEL OF TEACHING READING

Too often, the deficit model of teaching reading is used for years with at-risk readers. In this model, students are taught through their weakest modality, and their strengths are largely ignored. Some small gains may be made over time, but the large reading gains produced by strength teaching can be lost. Even worse, the students often struggle terribly in the process and feel stupid.

One common practice in this model is to teach students who are weak auditorially with intensive, systematic phonics instruction. When these students fail repeatedly to learn phonics, they are likely to be given remedial phonics! What is not understood is that many of these children *can learn to read*. They simply have difficulty learning phonics.

The deficit model of teaching reading is the opposite of the learning styles model. Most important, research tells us that teaching to the natural strengths and interests of at-risk readers has enabled these youngsters to make high reading gains (Anglin, 1996; Barber, Carbo, & Thomasson, 1998; Brooks, 1991; Carbo, 1978a, 1978b; Dunn, Griggs, Olson, Gorman, & Beasley, 1995; Hodgin & Wooliscroft, 1997; LaShell, 1986; Oglesby & Suter, 1995; Skipper, 1997; Snyder, 1997, 1994).

MATCHING READING METHODS
TO GLOBAL/ANALYTIC STYLES

It's extremely important to understand how to teach reading to global learners, because that tends to be the reading style of young children and at-risk readers (Dunn, Griggs, Olson, Gorman, & Beasley, 1995; Oexle & Zenhausern, 1981; Thies, 1999/2000). To teach global learners well, *meaning* is the key. Global students *need* to be deeply interested in what they're reading. While all students benefit from high-interest reading materials, strongly global students often *require* these kinds of materials to do their best. These youngsters recall words presented within the context of a high-interest story much more easily than through a story in which they have little interest. They also recall high-interest, dissimilar words (e.g., "dinosaur," "birthday") better than the low-interest, similar words commonly found in phonics materials (e.g., "jet," "met," "bet") (Burton, 1980).

Global students also tend to be strong visually and often need to "draw" mental pictures to help them remember. Their learning is hindered if the task cannot be visualized (Oexle & Zenhausern, 1981). Based on what we know about global youngsters, their reading programs should focus on high-interest stories (with recordings, if needed), words learned primarily in context, and reading skills that are drawn from the stories read, preferably taught in a game format. On the other hand, analytic students learn easily when some of their reading program is highly organized and builds the bits and pieces of reading into a whole. This topic is discussed in detail below.

THE ANALYTIC MODEL OF TEACHING READING

The analytic model of teaching reading moves from the parts to the whole, in the same way that phonics is taught (see Figure 5.2). The first stage of this model requires the mastery of isolated letter sounds. In Stage 2, students practice letter sounds by reading words that contain the learned sounds. Next they read connected text, or stories with words containing the learned sounds. The analytic model regards knowledge of letter sounds as a critical first skill for all learners.

Phonics: Who Succeeds and Who Fails?

Students who can learn phonics easily tend to be auditory/analytic learners. Strongly auditory students can hear and remember letter sounds easily. If they are also analytic, the logic of phonics makes good sense to them, for their style proceeds naturally from bits of information to the whole. Phonics instruction is usually highly sequential, organized, direct, and predictable—all conditions that appeal to analytics.

But phonics can be confusing and boring to strongly global students who don't learn easily when information is presented in small pieces, step by step.

Figure 5.1   Accommodating Reading Styles

Visual	Students With Perceptual Strengths Can Easily:	Enjoy/Learn Best by:	Learn to Read Best:
	• Recall what they see • Follow written or drawn instructions • Learn by observing people, objects, pictures, etc.	Using computer graphics; performing visual puzzles; looking at or designing maps, charts, graphs, diagrams, cartoons, posters, bulletin boards	With sight methods, dissimilar words, silent reading, words accompanied by pictures
Auditory	• Recall what they hear • Follow spoken instructions • Learn by listening and speaking	Talking, interviewing, debating, participating on a panel, asking and answering questions, memorizing, making oral reports	With phonics, choral reading, by listening to stories and recordings of books, discussing stories, reading orally
Tactile	• Recall what they touch • Follow instructions they write or touch • Learn by touching or manipulating objects	Doodling, sketching, playing board games, building models, constructing dioramas and relief maps, setting up experiments, writing, tracing	With writing/tracing methods, such as Fernald, language experience. By playing games or reading instructions, then making something
Kinesthetic	• Recall what they experience • Follow instructions that they perform or rehearse • Learn when engaged in physical activity	Playing floor games, assembling and/or disassembling objects, building models, participating in fairs, setting up experiments, acting, role playing, scavenger hunts	By pantomiming, acting in plays, riding a stationary bike while listening to a book, reading instructions and then building/doing something
Global	Tendencies Often: • Make decisions based on emotions and intuition • Are spontaneous, random • Focus on creativity • Care less about a tidy environment	Enjoy/Learn Best With: Information presented in an interesting or humorous story, examples, interesting materials, group work, and activities	Learn to Read Best: With holistic reading methods, such as recorded books, story writing, assisted reading methods, projects, and games
Analytic	Often: • Make decisions based on logic or common sense • Plan and organize well • Focus on details and facts • Like a tidy environment	Information presented in sequential steps, with rules and examples, structured materials, teacher-directed lessons, clear goals and requirements	Phonics (if auditory), programmed materials, puzzles, some worksheet—reinforced by strategies appropriate for global learners

SOURCE: © Marie Carbo, 1995.

Figure 5.2   The Analytic Model of Teaching Reading

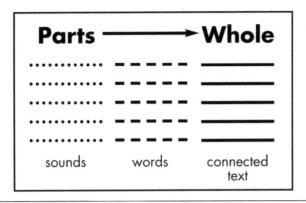

Teachers need to be careful that their strongly global students don't become lost in the details of phonics. By far the most serious problems, however, arise for students who are not sufficiently auditory to learn and blend letter sounds. If children cannot hear the differences among letter sounds, then they struggle to associate those sounds with their corresponding letters. At its worst, this situation is similar to that of a person who is tone deaf. No matter how many times that person tries to sing a song, he or she simply cannot sing it on key. Unfortunately, sometimes students with severe auditory weaknesses receive extra and more formalized phonics instruction year after year, which only makes them feel more hopeless and inadequate.

THE GLOBAL MODEL OF TEACHING READING

The global model of reading moves from the whole (the story) to the parts (words and then sounds within words) (see Figure 5.3). In the first stage, stories are read aloud to students repeatedly. After the children can read some stories or parts of stories independently, they move to Stage 2, where they practice some of the words and phrases taken from the stories they can read. In the last stage, the teacher helps the children study words from the stories that contain specific patterns. Words containing the same patterns are added so that students begin to understand the underlying phonic rules.

Holistic Methods: Who Succeeds and Who Fails?

All students need experiences with holistic reading methods because these methods emphasize the reading of a wide variety of high-interest materials. The reading style that is most responsive to a global approach is

Figure 5.3   The Global Model of Teaching Reading

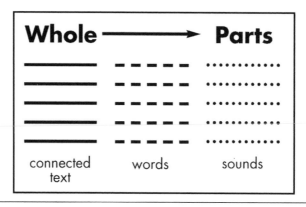

SOURCE: © National Reading Styles Institute, 1997.

that of the global, visual, and tactile learner. Holistic reading programs generally emphasize literature, reading for pleasure, phonics patterns, hands-on learning, and peer interaction—all of which appeal to global learners. These youngsters can recall words they see and hear repeatedly in high-interest books and stories. Story writing helps tactile learners to remember words they have felt as they write them.

But holistic reading programs can feel somewhat haphazard, especially to strongly auditory/analytic learners. If the modeling of stories is too infrequent or if the teacher does not provide sufficient repetition and systematic teaching, these youngsters can fall behind. And if structured phonics is not emphasized sufficiently, auditory/analytic students may not develop the tools they need for decoding words.

Finally, strategies such as invented spelling may confuse analytic students, who generally want to use correct spellings, or children with memory deficits, who sometimes persist in their invented spellings long past the early grades. Even students with good memories may have difficulty transitioning to traditional spellings if invented spelling is used for too long. Again, fit the program to the child, not the child to the program.

PENDULUM SWINGS HURT STUDENTS

Pendulum swings in reading instruction are predictable, and so is their direction. When an analytic approach like phonics has been popular for a time, the pendulum then swings over to a more global approach, such as choral reading, whole word, or whole language (which emphasizes the use of global reading methods). Some advocates of either approach continue to have heated debates. Those who believe fervently in global approaches to reading usually disbelieve in analytic approaches passionately—and vice versa. Strong emotions prevent rational, reasoned decisions about what is best for each student.

These pendulum swings are not new. For more than a century, educators have been searching for *the* single best way to teach reading. No matter which approach to teaching reading enjoys popularity, reading failures persist, disillusionment spreads, and the pendulum swings to yet another approach. At the turn of the last century, choral reading was used extensively. During the 1920s to the late 1930s, phonics gained in popularity. Then the look-say method (whole word) held sway for about 30 years (1940–1970). Next the pendulum swung back to phonics for about 20 years (1970–1990). In the early 1990s, whole language gained a strong foothold. Within several years, though, whole language was strongly criticized, especially by advocates of direct teaching and structured phonics.

Now, in the early years of the twenty-first century, reading educators are advocating a "balanced literacy" approach. However, given today's large amount of time-consuming paperwork, phonics, phonemics, skill work, test preparation, and testing, the pendulum has in reality swung back to an overemphasis on analytic approaches and materials, with little attention paid to identifying and accommodating students' strengths.

DIGGING DEEPER: SELECTING READING METHODS THAT ACCOMMODATE GLOBAL/ANALYTIC STYLES AND MODALITY STRENGTHS

As I mentioned above, many students have many learning strengths and are able to learn with a wide variety of reading methods. But for those youngsters with severe weaknesses, it is particularly important to accommodate their global or analytic style and modality strength(s). For example, the phonic, Orton-Gillingham, and linguistic methods are a good match for strongly analytic/auditory learners, while the whole-word, language-experience, Fernald, and recording methods better accommodate global/visual learners. Figure 5.4 provides an overview of reading methods with the styles they match. Each reading method and the reading style it matches is discussed below.

ANALYTIC READING METHODS

Phonic Method

Generally, students are taught to associate letters and their sounds in a prescribed sequence. After specific sounds are mastered, those letters are blended to form words. Then students learn additional sounds and learn to

Figure 5.4   Selecting Reading Methods That Accommodate Students' Reading Styles

Reading Method	Description	Reading Style Requirements
Phonics	Isolated letter sounds or letter clusters are taught sequentially and blended to form words.	Auditory and analytic strengths
Linguistic	Patterns of letters are taught and combined to form words.	Auditory and analytic strengths
Orton-Gillingham	Method consists of phonics plus tactile stimulation in the form of writing and tracing activities.	Auditory and analytic strengths combined with visual weaknesses
Whole-Word	Before reading a story, new words are presented on flash cards and in sentences with accompanying pictures.	Visual and global strengths
Language-Experience	Students read stories that they write.	Visual, tactile, and global strengths
Fernald	Students use language-experience method and trace over new words with index finger of writing hand.	Tactile and global strengths combined with visual weaknesses
Individualized Method	Students read books of their choice silently while the teacher holds individual conferences with students.	Visual and global strengths
Recorded Book	Students listen two to three times to brief recordings of books, visually track the words, then read the selection aloud.	Visual and global strengths

SOURCE: © Marie Carbo, 1987.

decode new and more complex words. That procedure continues until the student masters all the sounds of individual letters and some letter groups. Beginning books that have a phonic emphasis use a controlled vocabulary that contains the sounds students have been taught in separate lessons. Whole-class and small-group instruction are used often. Instruction proceeds in small, discrete, sequential steps, and youngsters are expected to keep pace with their group. Students are encouraged to decode unknown words independently.

Matches: strong analytic, strong auditory style
Mismatches: minimal analytic or weak auditory style

Orton-Gillingham Method (multisensory phonics)

This method uses a great deal of tactile reinforcement to teach phonics. It was developed to help students with dyslexia, who see moving and distorted letters. With the Orton-Gillingham method, both the sound and name of each letter are learned individually in a highly controlled, specified sequence. First the child sees the letter to be learned and hears the sound that it represents. Then the youngster traces over the letter with his or her finger and writes the letter (Gillingham & Stillman, 1968; Orton, 1937).

Note: If colored overlays lessen a student's visual problems, then reading methods that use tracing techniques to compensate for a student's visual problems may be unnecessary, i.e., Fernald and Orton-Gillingham.

Matches: strong analytic, strong auditory, and weak visual style
Mismatches: minimal analytic, weak auditory, or strong visual style

Linguistic Method

The linguistic method differs from phonics in that isolated letters are not stressed. Instead, letter clusters, patterns, or word "families" are taught, e.g., *fat, mat, cat, bat*. Word patterns are presented in a special sequence, and students are encouraged to decode new words using their knowledge and understanding of those patterns (Bloomfield, 1942; Fries, 1962). Beginning books and storybooks contain a highly controlled vocabulary with many words similar both in sound and configuration, as can be seen in this excerpt from a linguistic preprimer reader:

The man can fan.
I can fan the man.
The man can fan Dan.
I can fan Dan.

(Rasmussen & Goldberg, 1964, p. 3)

Note: The linguistic method focuses on learning *word patterns*, whereas the phonics method focuses on learning and blending isolated letter sounds.
  Matches: strong analytic, strong auditory style
  Mismatches: minimal analytic, weak auditory style

GLOBAL READING METHODS

Whole-Word Method (also called the "sight" method or "look-say")

In the whole-word method, story words that might be unfamiliar to students are taught before the students read the story. The words might be presented on flash cards, on the board, on charts, and so on. The students look at, listen to, and repeat the new words until they can read them quickly by sight. Students are encouraged to decipher an unknown word

Figure 5.5   This young boy is tracing a word in salt, one of the tactile strategies used in the Orton-Gillingham reading method.

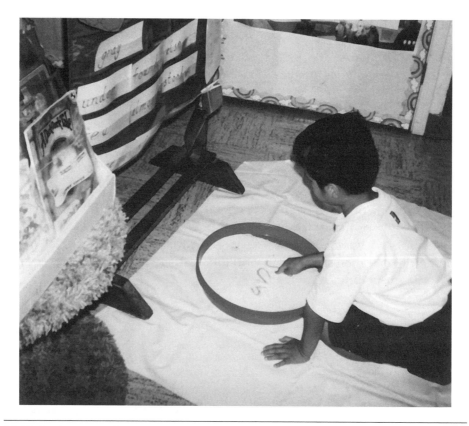

SOURCE: Courtesy of Anthon Elementary School, Uvalde, TX.

by looking at the word carefully, and using accompanying pictures and context as clues to the words. New words are introduced in a specific sequence with the repetition of words highly controlled.

Matches: moderate global, strong visual style
Mismatches: minimal global, weak visual style

Language-Experience Method

With this reading method, the student writes and reads his or her own stories. During the readiness phase, students often draw pictures and dictate a sentence or two for their teacher to write below their picture. At this stage, the children are not necessarily expected to read back their sentences, but some can and do. The purpose is to help students to associate printed and spoken words.

As the students mature, they begin to dictate sentences to their teacher on a topic of interest, often something that the group has experienced together, for example, going on a nature walk or talking to a visiting author. The teacher usually writes down the story sentences that the group dictates on a large chart or on the chalkboard. These short stories are often read aloud using the shared reading and choral reading methods (described in Chapter 6). Sometimes the students join in and read the story along with the teacher as it is being written. Many stories are written this way, and the teacher may accumulate the story charts into a book of stories created by the students.

After the students have composed a number of stories as a group and developed an initial sight vocabulary, they begin to write and read their own stories. Usually these are written daily on topics of interest provided by either the teacher or the students. Words are controlled only by the student's own speaking vocabulary and writing interests (Ashton-Warner, 1963; Goodman & Goodman, 1979). When a child cannot spell a word needed for a story, he or she may ask the teacher or a peer for help. Boxes containing words needed for writing, word walls, and dictionaries usually are available.

Matches: strong to moderate global, visual, tactile style
Mismatches: minimal global, weak visual, weak tactile style

Fernald Word-Tracing Method

This method is similar to the language-experience method but provides additional tactile reinforcement. It was developed to help students with visual problems. Note: If colored overlays help the student, tracing methods such as Fernald and Orton-Gillingham may be unnecessary.

When a youngster cannot spell a word needed for a story he or she is writing, the teacher writes the word on a large card by pressing down hard with a crayon to form raised, waxy letter surfaces. (For very young writers, write the word on construction paper. Otherwise, unlined 5" × 8" cards work well.) After the teacher writes the word, the student traces over it with his or her index finger a few times while saying the word; short words are said in a natural way, while long words are stated in syllables. Then the youngster turns the card over and writes the word into his or her story from the tactile memory of the word.

Grace Fernald found that "the child stops tracing when he is able to learn without it" (Fernald, 1943, p. 41). She also recommended the use of cursive writing as early as possible to help children experience the flow of the complete word, and to lessen "b" and "d" reversals. After the student writes a story, the teacher types it and places the typed copy next to or below the student's handwritten version. The student reads the typed copy within 24 hours of writing the story to help associate the typed words— which closely resemble the print found in books—with the student's own handwritten words.

Matches: strong to moderate global, weak visual, strong to moderate tactile style
Mismatches: minimal global, strong visual, weak tactile style

Individualized Method

This method is a formalized version of sustained silent reading. As in SSR, periods of time are set aside during the school day when students spend time reading (10–20 minutes for beginning readers, and about 30–45 minutes for experienced readers). Students can select from a wide range of reading choices including books, magazines, newspapers, and short stories. Most students are encouraged to spend some of their time reading books and short stories.

The teacher's role differs markedly from SSR, however. During SSR, the teacher reads a book while the students also read. When the individualized method is used, the teacher spends this time holding individual conferences with students. During the individual student conference, the student usually reads aloud a portion of his or her book to the teacher. The teacher keeps a record of how the student has read, records the student's reading errors, asks questions about the story, and notes any difficulty that the student is experiencing. Most student conferences take about five minutes so that the entire class can meet individually with the teacher during one week. Later, the teacher organizes the students into flexible groups that need to practice specific reading skills, and works with those groups during another time of the school day.

Matches: strong to moderate global, strong to moderate visual style
Mismatches: weak visual style

Carbo Recording Method

This method is similar to the individualized reading method, except that the reading material is recorded in small amounts with a special slow pace and chunked phrases (Carbo, 1978a, 1989, 1992). Students listen to a few minutes of a book or short story at least two times, and then read a portion back to their teacher and discuss what they have read. The method can also be used with individuals or with groups of students at listening centers. Chapter 7 describes the method in detail.

Matches: strong to moderate global, strong to moderate visual style
Mismatches: weak visual style

FOCUS ON THE STRENGTHS OF THE READER

Since young children and most at-risk readers tend to be global, tactile, and kinesthetic learners, an extensive body of learning styles and reading styles research supports the use of global reading approaches (with lots of hands-on skill teaching) as a framework for reading instruction—but only as a framework. The strategies within that framework depend on the reading styles of the group and of the particular students within that group. In general, reading instruction for at-risk readers should focus on the use of assisted reading methods, high-interest stories, skills taught in games, choices of reading materials, and writing activities. Small amounts of targeted phonics instruction are also important for most students.

IDENTIFYING READING STYLES WITH THE READING STYLE INVENTORY

Let's now apply the information in Chapter 4 to Melinda, analyze her case study, and then look at the information provided by her Reading Style Inventory® (RSI; Carbo, 1982, 1992).

Melinda hasn't done well in school for many years. Her strengths and weaknesses are described in the following case study. As you read about Melinda, jot down any clues about her global or analytic style and modality preferences, which reading method or methods you might try with her, and any other strategies that you think might help her.

> Melinda is having difficulty in school, and her teacher is very concerned about her. Melinda reads several years below grade level. She never seems to complete an assignment and experiences difficulty transferring anything from the board to her paper or from a textbook to her notes. Her spelling is poor. When writing, she often omits or reverses letters and has a great deal of difficulty sounding out words. Melinda is creative, outgoing, very sociable, and animated. It would be a shame to fail or retain her.

Does Melinda have the characteristics of a global or an analytic learner? What are her modality strengths or weaknesses? Before reading any further, take a moment to write down your analysis. Then proceed.

Based on the brief description, we can say tentatively that Melinda seems to be a strong global learner with serious visual problems (possibly visual dyslexia), as well as auditory weaknesses. Extreme weaknesses in both the visual and auditory modalities usually can cause extreme reading problems.

But there is hope for Melinda! First, whenever there is a possibility that a student has visual dyslexia, experiment with colored overlays to see if there is a color that will help to stabilize the printed words on a page for that student (see Chapter 10). Next, use observation techniques and checklists to help determine the child's reading style strengths and weaknesses.

For the most complete information, let's take a look at Melinda's RSI profile. This profile provides detailed information about Melinda's reading style, what accommodations she needs, and which reading strategies are recommended specifically for her.

What Melinda's Reading Style Inventory Tells Us

For our purposes here, we'll use Melinda's Condensed RSI Individual Profile (Figure 5.6). This profile, just one page in length, provides useful information for writing IEPs and for helping Melinda learn to read. (See Appendix E for more information about the RSI.) As we suspected, Melinda is a child of extremes. She is strongly global but only minimally analytic. She is strongly tactile and kinesthetic, but she is weak both visually and auditorially. There are many good strategies that will help Melinda learn to read, and the sooner these strategies are implemented, the better. Melinda is already years behind in reading.

Melinda's RSI Condensed Profile recommends her top three reading methods, top three reading materials, top five teaching strategies, and top five modifications. The reading methods recommended for Melinda are Fernald (she is weak visually and strong tactilely—a good match for Fernald), Carbo recordings (she is strong globally), and modeling methods. All of the methods recommended for Melinda are global, high interest, provide repetition, and will stretch Melinda with increasingly higher-level reading materials quickly.

Melinda's recommended reading interventions include recorded readings, hands-on activities, and large-muscle movement. The list of strategies tells us how to teach Melinda and includes the use of colored overlays (to reduce her visual problems), floor games (she's kinesthetic), hands-on games (she's tactile), and humor and stories (she's global). Her modifications include: the use of cursive writing to lessen her "b" and "d" reversals; the use of an index card under the words as she reads; limiting her board copying (she has difficulty doing this); use of colored overlays; and not requiring her to sound out words while reading if she has great difficulty doing this. (Remember, Melinda is weak auditorily. When she

Figure 5.6   Condensed RSI Individual Profile

Student Name: Melinda W.   **Grade:**   3rd
Date: 2004-12-13   **Teacher's Name:** Ms. Tillman

Global/Analytic Tendencies
   Very strong global tendencies
   Minimal analytic tendencies

Perceptual Strengths
   Minimal auditory strengths
   Minimal visual strengths
   Good tactile strengths
   Excellent kinesthetic strengths

Recommended Reading Methods
   Fernald Method
   Carbo Recorded-Book Method
   Modeling methods

Recommended Reading Materials
   Manipulatives w/large-muscle movement, floor games
   Index cards, writing notebook, dark crayon, word box
   "Hands-on" activities, manipulatives, games

Recommended Teaching Strategies
   De-emphasize decoding
   Allow student demonstrations, use floor games
   Include writing, drawing, games
   Try colored overlays and large print
   Use humor, stories, games

Special Modifications for This Student
For all reading methods, the following modifications are recommended for this student:
   Write directions for work, give to student
   Use cursive to lessen b and d reversals
   Provide repetition of words through many senses
   Do not have student sound out words while reading
   Limit board copying, give written copy of assignment
   Try colored overlay over page

SOURCE: © National Reading Styles Institute, 2005.

struggles to sound out words while reading, her comprehension is likely to suffer, and she is also likely to struggle and feel stressed—not good results if we want to release her natural learning power and teach the way she will learn most easily.) A good strategy for Melinda is to read parts of a story to her before she reads it, using the assisted reading methods.

Figure 5.7   This card summarizes Nancy's reading style. She prefers quiet (no talking), music, dim light, informal design. She is an auditory/visual learner, prefers some intake (food and drink), likes to read in the evening, needs little mobility, and is an analytic learner.

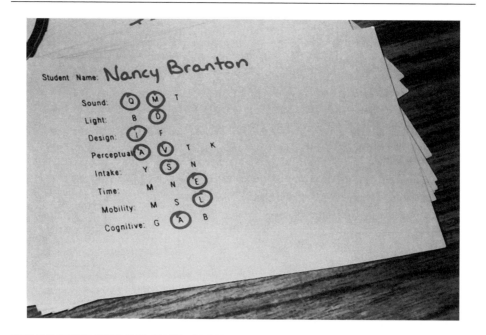

SOURCE: Photo by Diana Rigamonti. Courtesy of O'Connor Elementary School, Victoria, TX.

IN THE NEXT CHAPTER . . .

We'll look at a group of powerful reading methods called "assisted reading methods." I've organized them into a Continuum of Assisted Reading Methods so that you can select the most appropriate method or methods for your students. Used correctly, this group of methods can significantly increase reading fluency, vocabulary, comprehension, and enjoyment. After examining the continuum and each reading method, we'll apply them to five case studies of students.

6

Use the Continuum of Assisted Reading Methods

In this chapter, I describe a group of powerful reading methods known as "assisted reading methods." Great teachers of reading use these methods with ease and fluidity, especially with emerging and at-risk readers.

Let's begin with two classroom scenes. In the first scene, Sarah's reading group meets, and she's asked to read aloud. Sarah tries but can't read most of the words. She feels stupid and embarrassed. Later, Sarah tries paired reading with a classmate; they spend 10 minutes taking turns reading, both stumbling and missing many words, accomplishing very little except to provide poor reading models for one another. Across the hall, in the second classroom, Eduardo stares at a book during sustained silent reading (SSR), pretending that he is reading. He pretends to read in school—all day, every day—and hopes that he won't be called on to read.

Both Sarah and Eduardo need to work with the correct assisted reading methods. When they do, they will read with greater fluency and ease, and make substantial gains in reading. Before we help these children, let's find out more about assisted reading methods: what they are, why they work, and how to use the Continuum of Assisted Reading Methods.

THE POWER OF ASSISTED READING METHODS K–12

The idea behind assisted reading methods is simple and powerful. Students who are not yet independent readers, especially those reading well below their potential, need frequent modeling of high-interest reading materials. By modeling, I mean that a competent reader reads aloud a portion of a high-interest, somewhat challenging story, while the less-able reader listens to and looks at the words being read. If done correctly, after several repetitions of this process, the less-able reader is usually able to read back the passage with good fluency and comprehension.

IMPORTANCE OF READING FLUENCY

Assisted reading methods do a good job of significantly increasing reading fluency, and we definitely want our students to be fluent readers who can read rapidly, accurately, and with good expression. Here's why: when students read rapidly and accurately, it frees the brain to attend to the *meaning* of what is being read. Good readers are good comprehenders because their brains are always working and thinking while they read. They are *active and purposeful readers.*

Put another way, everyone has a limited amount of attention available when reading. If a great deal of attention is expended trying to decode words, less is available to understand what is being read (LaBerge & Samuels, 1974; Perfetti, 1985; Stanovich, 1980). The correct use of assisted reading methods provides the scaffolding that emerging and at-risk readers need to *bypass* the decoding process, read fluently, and concentrate on meaning.

Figure 6.1   Effective Fluency Instruction . . .

- makes word recognition automatic and effortless
- emphasizes rhythm and expression

PROBLEMS CAUSED BY INSUFFICIENT MODELING

Many youngsters in the early grades simply do not receive the amount and kind of modeling they need to become fluent readers. They are pushed along too fast. Children who are barely able to read often spend a great deal of time engaged in paired reading, where (like Sarah in the example that opened this chapter) they may be listening to another child who can barely read. Or (like Eduardo) they may sit quietly during sustained silent reading with a book in front of them that they cannot read, trying to do what they are not yet able to do: read independently books that interest them. At a time in their school career when they desperately need to hear and see good reading being modeled, they don't receive it. When these students reach middle or high school, they are often years behind in reading and still do not receive the modeling they require to move ahead.

THE CONTINUUM OF ASSISTED READING METHODS

There are many kinds of assisted reading methods. To show their relationship and purpose, I've created the Continuum of Assisted Reading Methods (Figure 6.2). Those methods that provide the most assistance to the reader are at the base of the model. Moving from the bottom to the top of the Continuum, each method provides increasingly less assistance or modeling. The strategies at the bottom, which provide the most assistance, are most appropriate for beginning readers and at-risk readers.

At the very top of the Continuum is our goal: sustained silent reading (SSR). During SSR the student receives no modeling of the text. What is modeled by the teacher and other students is the actual act of reading alone silently. That is why SSR is often ineffective for at-risk readers, especially those reading far below their grade level. At-risk readers need to raise their reading levels quickly; they need to see and hear good reading modeled so they can improve their reading—thus the use of the methods at the bottom of the Continuum. As students' reading ability improves, they need less assistance and can move up the Continuum, finally benefiting from SSR.

When the Continuum is used correctly, these two important reading goals are accomplished for students, especially emerging and at-risk readers:

- They can work with and read fluently higher-level, more interesting reading materials.
- When they read aloud, they feel and sound like competent, fluent readers.

In other words, use of the Continuum enables students to read increasingly difficult reading material so that their reading level increases rapidly. And, since sufficient modeling of a text before reading is provided, they are able to read it easily, without stress. Obviously, we don't want youngsters to struggle and stumble as they read in front of their peers (this experience is, almost without exception, the worst memory of adults who were at-risk readers as children).

Figure 6.2   Continuum of Assisted Reading Methods

The goal of the assisted strategies on this continuum is reading alone with ease and enjoyment (SSR). Moving from bottom to top, each strategy requires increasingly more reading independence of the student and less modeling by the teacher. Teachers should select the strategy that is most appropriate for a student or a group. Generally, strategies that provide the most modeling should be used with beginning readers and those who cannot read a particular text with good fluency.

Low Teacher Involvement
High Student Independence

Sustained Silent Reading

Each person in the classroom, including the teacher, reads alone. The time period for a group can range from about 10 to 45 minutes per session. A strong emphasis is placed on self-selection of reading materials and reading for pleasure.

Paired Reading

Two students take turns reading a passage or story. Teachers may pair youngsters of similar or dissimilar reading abilities and/or interests, or children may select partners.

Choral Reading

Two or more students read a passage in unison. Less-able readers try to follow the reading model provided by the more adept readers in the group.

Echo Reading

After discussing a passage, the teacher reads it aloud while the student (or group) follows along in the text. Then the teacher reads aloud a small portion, i.e., a sentence or paragraph, and the student reads it back. This procedure continues until the passage is completed.

Recorded Books

The youngster listens one or more times to a word-for-word recording while following along in the text, and then reads it aloud. Less-able readers can listen one to three times to two- to five-minute segments recorded at a slower-than-usual pace, and then read the passage aloud (Carbo 1989).

Neurological Impress

The teacher sits behind the youngster and reads into the child's ear. Both hold the book and read in unison. The teacher places his or her finger under the line of print being read by the teacher. The purpose is reading fluency.

Shared Reading

A high-interest book, often enlarged and containing many pictures and predictable language, is placed in front of students. The teacher reads the story while pointing to the words and pausing to ask questions. After a few readings, youngsters are encouraged to read along with the teacher.

High Teacher Involvement
Low Student Independence

SOURCE: © Marie Carbo, 1993.

Figure 6.3   The goal of the Continuum is sustained silent reading (SSR), reading silently, alone.

SOURCE: Photo courtesy of Roosevelt Elementary School, Medford, OR.

Amount and Kind of Modeling Provided by the Assisted Reading Methods

Each of the assisted reading methods models good reading. Different amounts and kinds of modeling are provided by each method. Since the methods at the base of the Continuum provide the most modeling, let's begin there.

Storytelling and Reading Aloud

These two strategies are not on the Continuum because they are not actually considered assisted reading methods. They are, however, extremely important techniques, especially for youngsters who have heard few stories and been read to very little in their lives (Trelease, 2006). Storytelling models good oral language for children; reading a story aloud helps to familiarize children with written language, which often has a different structure and vocabulary from the students' spoken language. We definitely want our students to become familiar with written language; that familiarity will make it easier for them to learn to read. That's why it's very important that teachers set aside time for reading aloud to their students, about 10–15 minutes *at least* twice daily for emerging and at-risk readers. For secondary teachers, read aloud to students about ten minutes per class period.

Shared Reading

Although this method is used extensively in the lower grades, it can easily be adapted for older students. Shared reading differs in important ways from reading aloud. When reading aloud, the reader looks at and reads words. The students cannot see the words; they just listen to what is being read. In shared reading, the students can see what is being read. Teachers might use a big book with enlarged print, poems or lists of words on the board or on charts, word walls, and so on (see Figure 6.4).

Figure 6.4   Maria Williams conducts a shared reading with her kindergartners. She uses a big book with large print that all the children can see, and points to the words as she reads them aloud.

SOURCE: Photo by Rosemarie Montejano. Courtesy of Margil Elementary School, San Antonio, TX.

Here is how shared reading is done: The reader points to the words with his or her finger or a pointer (a yardstick, for example), so that the students can hear the words *and see them* as they're being read. Initially, students are encouraged, but not expected, to read back. As they become familiar with the text, they are encouraged to read along with the reader.

For students who are just learning to read, it's recommended that the reader point to each word being read. In a short time (perhaps days, or weeks), the reader uses more of a sweeping motion above phrases as they are read. (The motion is above the phrases so that students can see the text that is going to be read.) Sometimes the reader pauses and asks questions about a story, such as: "How do you think the boy is feeling now?" or "What do you think will happen next?" A very short time may be allowed for student comments, and then the reader continues reading so that the flow of the story is not overly interrupted. This procedure is repeated several times over a few days, so that students hear and see the story repeatedly. As students are able, they join in and read along with the reader.

The major purposes of shared reading are to motivate students to read, to help them understand that writing proceeds from left to right, and to connect written and spoken language. This is all done in a relaxed setting, with lots of repetition for those youngsters who need it (Holdaway, 1979; Reutzel, Hollingsworth, & Eldredge, 1994).

Differentiating the Shared Reading Method

- To use the shared reading method with one student, sit next to the student with a regular-sized book and point to the words as you read them in the same manner as described above.
- If no big books are available and you want to use the method with a small group of students, hold a storybook so that it faces the students and they can see the words as you point to them. (You'll be reading the book with the words upside down to you.) This strategy will work only with storybooks that have print large enough for every child in the group to see.
- In the upper grades, use the shared reading method when reviewing notes on the chalkboard, on a poster or chart, or on an overhead transparency. This will help at-risk readers to understand what is written, and they will begin to remember some of the words. Generally, shared reading is not powerful enough to raise reading levels significantly for older students, but it will provide some help.

Neurological Impress Method

Neurological impress, which combines shared reading and choral reading, is done individually with students. This simple method enabled 24 students in Grades 7–10 to achieve a 1.9-year gain in reading comprehension in only six weeks. The students worked with the method just 15 minutes each day (Heckelman, 1969).

Here is how the method works: The reader sits next to (and slightly behind) the student. The student holds the book or story being read while the reader reads a few inches away from the student's ear and traces his or her finger under the words. The material should be read in an animated way that engages the student. The student choral-reads the material aloud with the reader, while seeing and hearing the words read. After a specified period of time (from five to 15 minutes), the activity is stopped.

Differentiating the Neurological Impress Method

- Use reading materials of great interest to the student. Provide choices and allow the student to select what will be read.
- Encourage the use of reading materials that challenge the student.
- If the student can't keep up, slow your pace.
- If the student still can't choral-read the material with you, choose something easier.
- If the student appears fatigued or can't sit for long, stop the activity or take a short break and return to the work.
- Some students may be embarrassed and may not want to read along with a teacher. In such a case, try the method that follows.

Figure 6.5   Two girls enjoy reading *Charlotte's Web* together—one needs the help of a recording; the other does not.

SOURCE: Photo courtesy of Robb Elementary School, Uvalde, TX.

Carbo Recording Method®

Like the neurological impress method, the Carbo Recording Method has produced high reading gains in short periods of time (Barber, Carbo, & Thomasson, 1998; Bradsby, Wise, Mundell, & Haas, 1992; Carbo, 1992; Molbeck, 1994; Morris, 2003; Queiruga, 1992). For example, elementary students with severe learning disabilities who were nonreaders or were reading up to five years below their reading level gained eight months in word recognition in three months (Carbo, 1978a). Tenth graders with disabilities who were reading six to 10 years below grade level made 2.2-year gains in reading comprehension in four months (Carbo, 1992; Queiruga, 1992), and at-risk high school students made gains of two years in reading comprehension in just seven weeks (Morris, 2003).

In this method, high-interest reading materials are recorded in very small amounts using a slightly slow pace and chunked phrases. Students look at the words and listen to the passage two or three times and then read the passage back. Generally, the student should be able to read the passage back with good expression and no more than two or three errors. Note: Chapter 7 describes this method in detail and provides many more suggestions for its use.

Differentiating the Carbo Recording Method

- If the student seems hesitant during the read-back, another repetition of the recording may be needed.
- If the reading material is too difficult, try something easier.
- Include recordings and stories at listening centers so groups can work together on the same story.

Figure 6.6   Mikkel, a sixth grader, understands and uses the Continuum to help a first grader improve his reading fluency and comprehension. Their teacher, Susanne Aabrandt, says of her program, "A wonderful side effect is that the students connect, make friends, and later share their love of reading together."

SOURCE: Photo by Susanne Aabrandt. Courtesy of Rosalund School, Vaerloese, Denmark.

Echo Method

This method can be used with any reading material, including text-books. Both the reader and student usually have a copy of the reading material. The reader reads a small amount of material, and the student then reads the same material back immediately. The amount being read could be one sentence, a few sentences, a paragraph, or a few paragraphs. The amount read should be small enough so that the student is able to read the material back with ease. Often this technique is used for just five to 15 minutes daily.

Differentiating the Echo Method

- For students who can't echo back one sentence, begin by reading the first part of the sentence (the student then echoes it back), then the next part of the sentence (the student echoes it back), and so on. Keeping the amount of material very small makes the task easier. If this strategy doesn't work, it may be that the reading material is just too difficult for the student and should be changed.
- The echo method can be used with a group of students. Read a short passage to the group. Each student sees and hears it, but only one student echoes it back. Each time a passage is read, a different student does the echo reading. If this technique creates any stress, have the students choral-read each passage back as a group. Hoffman (1987) described an adaptation of the echo method which he developed for use with a small group. The teacher begins by reading a story aloud. Next he or she reads the story paragraph by paragraph while the students read along *and* echo-read each paragraph. When the reading is complete, each child prepares to read one paragraph by practicing it repeatedly (repeated reading), and reads it aloud to the group. Hoffman's procedure is supported by research (Morris & Nelson, 1992; Reutzel & Hollingsworth, 1993; Reutzel, Hollingsworth, & Eldridge, 1994).
- Try the echo method with a textbook. If the material is difficult, start by reading just one sentence and have the entire group echo it back. Continue, slowly increasing the amount of material read.
- Try echo reading, using a textbook as the reading material for five minutes daily. In a short time, most students will become familiar with the terminology in the textbook and find it easier to echo it back. As the students become more proficient, allow them to volunteer to do the echo reading individually for just the last minute.
- Don't call on students to echo a reading unless they want to do it.
- If an individual student is hesitant to echo-read, try this: Read a sentence to the student. Then choral-read the sentence *with the student* to provide support. When the student is ready, allow him or her to do the echo reading alone.

Figure 6.7   This card reader is similar to the Echo reading method. First the youngster puts the card through the card reader and hears his teacher read what is written on the card. Then he records himself and compares his reading to his teacher's reading.

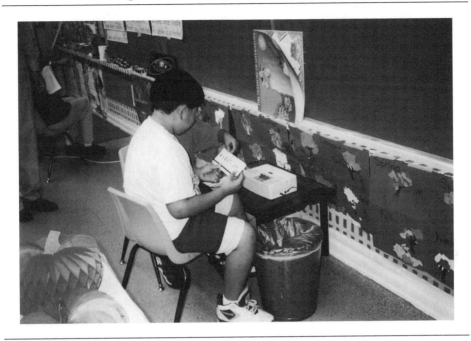

SOURCE: Courtesy of Robb Elementary School, Uvalde, TX.

Choral Reading Method

Choral reading is identical to shared reading, except that students are expected to read along with the reader immediately. As with shared reading, the reader uses his or her finger or a pointer to point to words while reading them. The pointer is placed above the words being read and is used in a sweeping motion. Choral reading is often used with a group to read big books, word walls, or any material large enough for a group to read.

Differentiating the Choral Reading Method

- The reader's voice can become stronger and softer during the reading. It should be stronger when the students are hesitant in their reading, and softer as their reading is strong. In other words, the reader does less when less is needed by the students, and more when they need more assistance.
- When students do any kind of individual read-back, join in and choral-read with them when their reading is very hesitant or shaky, if it seems appropriate to do so. As they become more confident, allow them to read alone.

- As students become stronger in their reading ability, they can choral-read together without a teacher's assistance.
- Use all the suggestions for differentiating instruction that are listed for shared reading and echo reading.

Paired Reading Method

In this method, two students take turns reading a portion of a book (usually a paragraph or page). With this method, each student reads a different part of a text independently. Little or no modeling is provided for the at-risk readers, unless one member of the pair is a good reader.

Differentiating the Paired Reading Method

- Pair a good reader with an at-risk reader. Have the good reader use the echo method (I read, and then you read the same passage back to me).
- Allow at-risk readers to choose what they would like to read from a group of acceptable choices.
- Set up a listening center with recordings of the books students will read using this method. Then students who need the modeling can listen to the recording while following along in the book *before* they attempt the same passage with a classmate.
- Two at-risk readers who are buddies can do paired reading together. Have them work with a Carbo recording of the reading material a sufficient number of times before they use this method together.

Sustained Silent Reading

Each student reads alone for a set period of time something that he or she wants to read. SSR is the goal of the Continuum.

USING THE CONTINUUM: FIVE CASE STUDIES

Now it's easy to understand why students like Sarah and Eduardo (whom I discussed at the beginning of this chapter) are not succeeding. They've been pushed upward on the Continuum too fast—like baby birds expected to fly before their wings are strong enough. Sarah and Eduardo are simply not yet ready to fly. They are capable neither of reading with another student (paired reading) nor of reading solo (sustained silent reading).

Students who don't read well, like Sarah and Eduardo, usually benefit from a great deal of modeling. They need to have many experiences with the methods toward the bottom of the Continuum (shared reading, neurological impress, Carbo recordings, and echo reading). This modeling will strengthen their oral language, sight vocabulary, and reading fluency. As their reading improves and they become more competent and confident readers, they'll be ready to practice reading with the help of good readers (choral reading, paired reading). Finally, they'll be able to spend more and more of their time reading alone. Now, let's help Sarah and Eduardo and the other students in the case studies below.

Case Study #1. Sarah, Elementary School

As you recall, Sarah had difficulty reading in her reading group and was stumbling and missing words during paired reading. Let's use the Continuum to help Sarah first. Sarah is unprepared to read with her reading group. She needs either to work with the neurological impress method with someone (a volunteer, a teacher, a peer, or an older student) or to work with a Carbo recording of the story. If a Carbo recording is used, ideally Sarah should listen to the entire story recorded at a regular pace, and then she should work with just a page or two of the story recorded with the Carbo method. In this way, she would understand the entire story and could participate in a discussion of it. She could also read aloud to her reading group any portion of the story that she practiced with the slow-paced, brief Carbo-style recording.

During paired reading, Sarah should be paired with a good reader who either echo-reads or choral-reads with her, depending on how much help Sarah needs. If echo reading were used, for example, her partner would read half a page to Sarah, who would then echo-read it back to her partner. They would continue in this way, with her partner reading first and Sarah echo-reading the same part of the story. (If half a page is too much, then Sarah's reading buddy should read just a sentence or two before Sarah echoes it back.)

Case Study #2. Eduardo, Elementary School

As you recall, Eduardo was doing what many older, at-risk readers do during SSR: *pretending* that he was reading a difficult book. During SSR, Eduardo needs to work with a Carbo recording of his story or book. Then he would be able to listen to a passage through his headset without disturbing his classmates; after sufficient repetitions, he would be ready to read some or all of the passage to his teacher or a volunteer. In this way, while Eduardo's classmates are reading independently, he is doing what he should be doing—improving his reading with the help of a powerful assisted reading method.

Case Study #3. Christopher, Middle School

Chris reads about two years below his grade level. Using small amounts of modeling, he could catch up if he spent *some time reading*, which he seldom does. Chris, who has been bored with standard reading materials for a long time, has decided that he just doesn't like to read. Our first step with Chris would be to find out if there is anything that he *does* like to read. He might be a candidate for exciting short stories with adventure, mystery, or science-fiction plots. If he likes comic books, then they should be used.

We need to find out what he would like to read before we can help him, and then use the method or methods on the Continuum that would be best suited to improving his fluency and comprehension. Since Chris is an older student, Carbo recordings would be a strong possibility.

Case Study #4. Margarita, Elementary School

Margarita is in second grade and can't track words. She has been placed on recordings but is unable to follow the text. We need to move down on the Continuum. Since Margarita can't track words, the reading methods used with her would need to *track the words for her,* until she learns how to do this herself. There are two such methods on the Continuum: shared reading and neurological impress. A good solution would be to train an older student or volunteer to use these methods with Margarita so that she can receive this modeling every day, if possible. During shared reading, her reader should point to each word. In a short while, Margarita should place her finger on top of the reader's finger as he or she tracks the words and reads aloud. As her skills improve, the neurological impress method can be used as well, since the teacher tracks the words for the student.

Case Study #5. Sam, High School

Sam is very far behind in his reading. He's in tenth grade and reading on a shaky first-grade level. His teachers tried the neurological impress method (a good choice), but Sam feels embarrassed by the process. He needs other assisted reading methods that will give him confidence, provide a great deal of modeling, and help to build his base of sight words. There are three good possibilities for Sam among the assisted reading methods: shared reading, Carbo recordings, and echo reading. Some shared reading and echo reading should be used first. Later, Sam's teacher might begin the recordings by asking Sam to dictate simple, short stories about himself (perhaps three or four sentences long). These stories can then be recorded for him. As his reading level rises, high-interest short stories not dictated by Sam can be recorded for him. Sam needs consistent modeling of stories that interest him *at least* four times weekly if his very large reading gap is to be closed.

Recommendations

- Teach volunteers to work with students who need the methods at the bottom of the Continuum.
- Teach capable parents to use certain methods at the base of the Continuum with their children at home (especially those students who are at risk).
- Replace periods of sustained silent reading with specific time for the Continuum. During this time, use the methods on the Continuum that provide a great deal of modeling (shared reading, neurological impress, Carbo, echo) with emerging and at-risk readers.

- For inclusion students and those for whom English is a second language, use the methods at the bottom of the Continuum often to improve their English and to increase reading fluency, comprehension, and vocabulary (Koskinea, et al., 1999).
- Before choral-reading a passage, place students on recordings that practice that passage so that they can "shine" in front of their peers during the actual choral reading.

Be Creative!

Use the Continuum of Assisted Reading Methods in creative ways. Combine methods when it makes sense to do so. For example, before children choral-read a passage, they might listen to a tape recording of it to

Figure 6.8   A fourth grader conducts a shared reading with two young children. Next, she will echo-read the story sentence by sentence with the children. Then they will choral-read together, and, finally, each student will read the story aloud. By moving up the Continuum in this way, these young children will receive the modeling they need to read the story fluently.

SOURCE: Courtesy of Benson Elementary School, Uvalde, TX.

improve their fluency. Or a teacher might echo-read a story with a small group, with group members choral-reading the material back to the teacher.

Great teachers of reading place their students in experiences that assure success. When students struggle as they read, try referring to the Continuum for help. Remember that assisted reading methods provide the modeling that many emerging and at-risk readers need. Students should spend most of their time using the methods that will help them move forward and achieve success rapidly.

IN THE NEXT CHAPTER . . .

We'll look at the Carbo recording method—what it is, why it works, and how to create your own recordings. Beginning readers and at-risk readers have made excellent gains with this method, with older students making the largest gains in short periods of time.

7

Use the Carbo Recording Method

W hen Georgette entered my classroom 30 years ago, I was stunned to discover that in her first three years of schooling she had learned to read only one word: "Georgette." This sweet little girl, who was repeating second grade, did have a severe memory deficit, but how was it possible that she had learned just one word in three years of schooling? After we worked together for one month, Georgette learned to read 31 words (Carbo, 1978b). It wasn't a miracle. It was the recording method I invented just for her that made the difference in her life.

After Georgette's great success, I chose eight of my most at-risk readers and decided that every night I would record whatever each student wanted to read. My second graders read on a primer level, and my fifth and sixth graders were reading three to five years below their grade level. After three months of working with the recordings, the group's average gain in word recognition was eight months (Carbo, 1978a).

My students had extreme auditory deficiencies, which made learning phonics very difficult for them. Some of them couldn't associate letters with their sounds; others couldn't distinguish between similar sounds, recall and blend sounds to form words, recall what they heard, and so on. Apparently, the strong emphasis on phonics in my district had blocked their learning. Everything changed when we worked together with the special recordings described in this chapter.

Figure 7.1   Georgette (the child for whom this recording method was created) practices reading her first book to a friendly doll named George.

SOURCE: Photo by Marie Carbo. Courtesy of the Robert W. Carbonaro School, Valley Stream, NY.

Tommy's transformation was the most amazing. Tommy was a bright sixth grader struggling to read on a *first-grade level*. He hated being labeled "special ed," hated reading, and would slink in and out of my resource center, hoping that no one would see him. On the first day of my experiment, Tommy asked me to record *Charlotte's Web* for him, which was at least three to four years above his reading level. I asked him to choose where he wanted me to begin. The part where Wilbur and Charlotte meet, he said. He may not have been able to read, but, like most kids, he knew what he liked.

The next day, Tommy listened to his recorded half-page of *Charlotte's Web* four times and sat down next to me. He read back the passage to me fluently. It was the single best day of my teaching career. Each day for the next three months, with the aid of my recording, Tommy moved forward another half-page in *Charlotte's Web*. Each day he read the recorded passage back to me with good fluency and expression, even imitating the voices I used for each character. I watched this formerly nervous, angry boy become more and more confident and motivated about learning to read. At the end of our trial, Tommy had gained 1.3 years in reading in just three months. He was on his way to becoming a lifelong reader.

What heartened me was how all eight children would enter my center so excited about reading the recorded book of their choice, and then conferencing with me. From the very first day of using the recordings, the children began to read more smoothly and confidently, and they improved in reading fluency and comprehension. This simple method of recording not only enabled my students to raise their reading abilities and test scores but made reading feel much easier for them as well. It was actually fun to read for the first time in their lives.

RESEARCH RESULTS

Many educators have reported that their students have made exceptionally high gains in reading fluency, vocabulary, and comprehension, as well as greatly improved attitudes toward reading and school (Barber, Carbo, & Thomasson, 1998; Bradsby, Wise, Mundell, & Haas, 1992; Carbo, 1992; Molbeck, 1994; Morris, 2003; Queiruga, 1992). Even students written off as unteachable have learned to read. Graduate student Angela Haller taught a child to read who was "missing about half his left hemisphere due to surgery for a brain tumor." Haller wrote in her report: "I have been excited to see him change. He truly enjoys reading now. There can be no doubt that the Carbo method is responsible for his success."

Repeatedly, teachers and researchers report an almost immediate improvement in their students' reading fluency and comprehension. Students hear themselves reading words they have never read before, words that used to stop them cold. They hear themselves reading material that is above their reading level with greater ease, better comprehension, and enjoyment. Best of all, the entire process feels—and is—relatively effortless.

DESCRIPTION OF THE METHOD

This method of recording differs from others in that *very* small amounts of text are recorded on one tape side or one CD track, at a slower than usual pace, with good expression. The student listens to the brief recorded passage while following along in the text, and then reads that passage, or a portion of it, aloud to the teacher, a peer, or a volunteer soon afterward. The method has enabled most at-risk readers to master and read back fluently passages that are well above their reading level.

In order to ensure that students will be able to read back a recorded passage with fluency and ease, the person making the recording needs to control these four variables: (1) the amount recorded, and his or her own (2) pace, (3) phrasing, and (4) expression.

The simple key is this: If the gap between the student's reading level and the level of the material is small, record between five and 15 minutes of a story on one tape side or CD track, at a fairly normal pace, with natural expression and phrasing. If the gap is large, use a slower pace, fewer words to a phrase, exaggerate your expression slightly, and record much less— about two to five minutes on a tape side or CD track.

Figure 7.2   Austin Renfro is thrilled after reading aloud his favorite recorded short story, "Big Cat and Little Cat."

SOURCE: Courtesy of West Amory Elementary School, Amory, MS.

The books and stories selected for recording should be somewhat *above* the student's reading level, and at or slightly above the student's language-comprehension level. (Well-written texts that are of great interest to students have produced the largest gains. Note: The Spelling and Grammar check feature of Microsoft Word will provide the grade level of a text and the Auto Summarize feature will highlight the main idea.) Because the material will be stretching them somewhat beyond their current level, most students will need to listen to the recording and follow along two or three times before being able to read back the material fluently. That's why only two to five minutes of text should be recorded on each tape side or CD track. Text is recorded in small, consecutive amounts. For example, pages 1–4 of a storybook might be on the first tape side or CD track, pages 5–8 on

Figure 7.3   How to Record for Maximum Reading Gains

- Use high-interest stories that are above the student's independent reading level.

- Record at a slow pace with good expression.

- Record about 2–4 minutes of text per tape side.

SOURCE: © National Reading Styles Institute, 2000.

the second, pages 9–11 on the third, and so on. Even a short picture book might take four tape sides or CD tracks to complete.

Recent research indicates that the reading problems of dyslexics may stem from their "inability to process the fast sounds of spoken words" (Blakeslee, 2005). The slow pace of this recording method enables students to keep the pace *and* to process the words being read. It also enables teachers to stretch students into higher materials that they would find too difficult if read at a normal pace.

Important note: You must secure written permission to record from the copyright holder of the book or story you wish to record. You may, however, record any material that is in the public domain. See for example http://publicdomain.com. For more information, see the short section on copyright at the end of this chapter.

How to Differentiate for Students With Special Needs

Let's look at how to differentiate the recordings for two very different students so that each learns to read and enjoys the process.

1. Robert. Robert is an eleventh grader reading on a primer level. His teacher began reading very easy books to him written at a primer level. Then she asked him to dictate stories to her that were simple, but interesting to him. His teacher wrote down and then recorded his first story of 10 words using this recording method; Robert listened to the story three times and read it back to her. Slowly, a bank of Robert's own recorded stories developed. Then he moved on to high-interest, recorded first-grade stories.

2. Isabel. Isabel's primary language is Spanish. Her English is limited. This is true of some of her classmates as well. Her teacher began by recording fairly easy stories for these children. For each story, she recorded an introduction in Spanish so that these youngsters could hear an overview of the story in their primary language. The rest of the story was recorded in English. Not only did the youngsters do a good job of reading back and understanding the stories, their understanding and use of English improved considerably.

Figure 7.4   After listening to the same passage twice, these students will discuss the passage with their teacher and then pair-read it.

SOURCE: Courtesy of Robb Elementary School, Uvalde, TX.

Figure 7.5   Under the bookshelf there is good lighting, a tape recorder, and a place to hang headsets. (The children are tracing over words from their reading.)

SOURCE: Courtesy of West Amory Elementary School, Amory, MS.

Why the Method Works

For many at-risk readers, there's a substantial time lag between when they see and are able to say many words. That lag produces slow, laborious reading, which greatly hinders comprehension. It's terribly difficult for students to recall what a passage is about when they have to expend so much effort figuring out each word. In effect, the recording does what the child is not yet able to do naturally: It verbalizes the printed word with the correct pace, phrasing, and expression. As a result, students make fewer reading errors, and the possibility of forming incorrect reading patterns is diminished.

The Recordings Are Brain-Friendly

According to brain research, these recordings enhance learning and recall because: (1) students can read high-interest, challenging reading material, so they're emotionally engaged; (2) the pace, chunking of phrases, and good expression are easy to follow and support comprehension; (3) the amount of text to be read is small, enabling students to master it in a few repetitions; (4) the task is multimodal; and (5) the students control the amount of repetition needed as well as when they will read aloud, so there is little or no stress (Caine, Caine, McClintic, & Klimek, 2005; Jensen, 1998; Sprenger, 1999, 2003) (see Figure 7.6).

Figure 7.6   Why the Carbo Method Works

- Meaning increases learning and comprehension.

- High-interest stories have high meaning to the brain.

- The brain is a pattern sorter.

- With sufficient modeling of the text, the brain *automatically* identifies word patterns and begins to decipher unknown words.

SOURCE: © National Reading Styles Institute, 2000.

Printed and Spoken Words Are Synchronized

The slow recordings synchronize for the reader the spoken words with the printed text, while the repetition of small amounts of text facilitates word retention. The short, natural phrases translate the printed page into meaningful segments, and the pauses help to increase word recognition and comprehension. In effect, the person who records the passage sets the pace for the reader, in much the same way as a metronome does for a musician. The recording provides a good, clear speech model.

Students Develop a Large Sight Vocabulary Quickly

Best of all, it's not necessary to record dull, simple reading materials to improve a student's sight vocabulary. In fact, words presented within high-interest contexts are easier to learn and retain than words presented in isolation or within a dull context. Since students can determine the number of repetitions needed, the student is in control of his or her own learning. Students can read rich, varied language with the assistance of the recordings, and they are able to read and enjoy stories that appeal to their interests. So they read more and more for pleasure, which speeds up the development of their sight vocabulary and understanding of words (Nagy, Anderson, & Herman, 1987; Stanovich, 2000; Sternberg, 1987; Swanborn & de Glopper, 1999).

Students learn common words presented repeatedly in the context of high-interest stories—words such as "like," "the," "a," "is," "it," "he," "can," "would," and so on. These words are much more difficult to learn out of context on flash cards. Figure 7.7 lists the 100 words used most frequently in written English. The first column of 25 words make up approximately *one-third of the words* that most of us will encounter in our reading. The entire list of 100 words represents *half the words* in most written materials.

When students listen to these special recordings, they add many words to their memory bank that they can read rapidly on sight. This sharp increase in sight vocabulary promotes reading comprehension development (Beck & McKeown, 1991). Since they know more sight words, their brain is freed to focus on just the few unknown words in a text. This enables students to read increasingly difficult material. After repeated work with the recorded texts, the brain *automatically* begins to identify more and more word patterns and to decipher more new words.

How the Student Works With the Recordings

Usually a student listens to a recording two or three times while following along in the book or story. As soon as possible, the youngster reads the passage aloud to someone and discusses it. The "someone" could be a teacher, parent, peer, or volunteer.

Note: It's not necessary for the student to read back an entire passage, but a sufficient amount should be read aloud to ensure that the youngster has mastered the text.

When a Student Cannot Read Back a Passage With Ease

After listening to a recording (usually two or three times), the student should be able to read back that passage fluently with no more than a few errors. Since every rule has its exceptions, there may be some strongly motivated students who make excellent progress with four repetitions of a recording. Generally, however, if a youngster needs more than three repetitions, the

Figure 7.7   100 Most Frequently Occuring Words in Printed Material

These are the most common words in English, ranked in frequency order. The first 25 make up about a third of all printed material. The first 100 make up about half of all written material. Is it any wonder that all students must learn to recognize these words instantly and to spell them correctly?

the	or	will	number
of	one	up	no
and	had	other	way
a	by	about	could
to	word	out	people
in	but	many	my
is	not	then	than
you	what	them	first
that	all	these	water
it	were	so	been
he	we	some	call
was	when	her	who
for	your	would	am
on	can	make	its
are	said	like	now
as	there	him	find
with	use	into	long
his	an	time	down
they	each	has	day
I	which	look	did
at	she	two	get
be	do	more	come
this	how	write	made
have	their	go	may
from	if	see	part

SOURCE: Reprinted with permission from John Wiley & Sons, Inc. *The Reading Teacher's Book of Lists*, Fifth Edition, by E. B. Fry & J. E. Kress. San Francisco, CA: Jossey-Bass, 2006.

story or book may be too difficult for that student, or it may be recorded incorrectly for that youngster. Choose easier reading material, reduce the amount of text that the student needs to master, or record at a slower pace if the pace is too fast.

How to Use the Same Recording With Students of Differing Abilities

If a student can read the story with ease without the recording, choose a more difficult book. If the youngster wants to listen to the tape and follow along for enjoyment, allow it, but encourage the student to move on to higher-level materials as soon as possible.

If the reading passage seems to be too difficult, so that even four repetitions do not enable the student to read back the passage, the possibility is either that the reading material is too difficult or that too much has been recorded on one tape side or CD track. In such a case, direct the student to listen to the entire recording once while following along, and then relisten two to three times more to just a small section at the beginning of the passage, such as the first paragraph or page. Then the student should read back just the portion listened to repeatedly, preferably to the teacher. If the read-back is still labored, then easier reading material should be selected.

Figure 7.8   Doug started at a primer reading level in the first year of Queiruga's Reading Lab. By May of that school year, he was reading on a sixth-grade level.

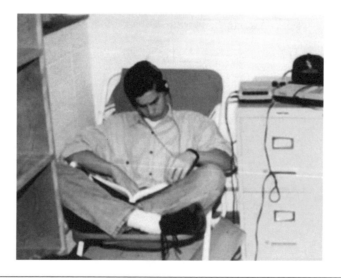

SOURCE: Photo by Linda Queiruga. Courtesy of Canyon del Oro High School, Tucson, AZ.

Figure 7.9   A student looks through envelopes containing Linda Queiruga's recorded short stories. The summer before the program started, Queiruga recorded over 240 high-interest short stories using this special recording method.

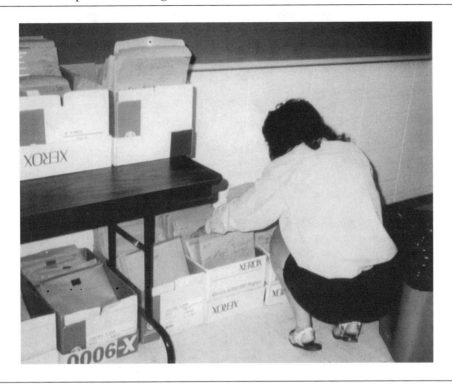

SOURCE: Photo by Linda Queiruga. Courtesy of Canyon del Oro High School, Tucson, AZ.

THE POWER OF READING LABS, ESPECIALLY FOR OLDER STUDENTS

Extraordinary success has resulted with the use of this recording method in reading labs, especially with older students. Gains of several years in reading in only a few months have been common, along with dramatically higher reading enjoyment, motivation, and confidence, as well as greatly improved student behavior.

Linda Queiruga's (1992) reading lab was the first outstanding model. Her 33 tenth-grade special education students began the program reading on second- and third-grade levels. After only four months of working 45 minutes daily with the recordings in Queiruga's lab, they made average gains of 2.2 years in reading comprehension on the Gates-MacGinitie Achievement Test. One boy who began that school year reading on a primer level gained six years in the first year of the recording program.

Figure 7.10   Mike made the highest gain in the first four months of Linda Queiruga's Reading Lab, gaining four years in reading vocabulary and comprehension on the Gates-MacGinitie Reading Achievement Test. Queiruga recorded many articles that her students requested. Mike's favorite articles were from *Field & Stream* magazine.

SOURCE: Photo by Linda Queiruga. Courtesy of Canyon del Oro High School, Tucson, AZ.

Queiruga recorded many short stories, ranging from third- to ninth-grade reading levels, with this special method. She placed each story with its tapes in an envelope, and labeled each envelope with the name of the story and the reading level. Each student was told his or her reading level and directed to work with stories at least one year higher than that level. After listening to a recorded story as many times as needed, each student then read a portion of the story aloud to Queiruga, provided an oral summary, and completed a few follow-up comprehension and vocabulary

Figure 7.11   Tony, a student with severe dyslexia, began tenth grade with almost unintelligible speech, struggling to read on a second-grade level. After three years of Carbo recordings, Tony graduated from high school reading on a seventh-grade level with much improved speech. He went on, with assistance, to complete two years of college. (Notice that Tony is learning to read an *Employee Handbook*, recorded for him by his teacher, Linda Queiruga.)

SOURCE: Photo by Linda Queiruga. Courtesy of Canyon del Oro High School, Tucson, AZ.

questions. This procedure freed the students to try increasingly difficult reading levels, challenge themselves, monitor their own progress, and move ahead at comfortable rates.

In its third year, Queiruga's lab served more than 200 at-risk readers. Many of the original group, who were potential dropouts, went on to college instead. During this process, Queiruga became a great reading teacher.

Figure 7.12   Grade 6 Reading Interests

- Scary books and stories
- Comics, cartoons, magazines about popular culture
- Books and magazines about sports, cars, and trucks
- Series books
- Funny books
- Books about animals

SOURCE: Adapted from Moorman & Turner, 1999.

A WORD OF CAUTION ABOUT WORD COUNTS

Stories with word counts have numbers to the left of every line, indicating how many words are in the story up to that point. In these days of too much testing, it's extremely important to be aware of how detrimental constant word counts can be for students.

Here's why: Remember that brain research tells us that memory and learning ability are enhanced when students are offered choices in their learning, are emotionally engaged in the material, and are free of stress. For best results, we want our students to focus their energies on *comprehension* and *reading enjoyment,* not on how many words they've read at their fastest speed. That kind of reading can remove the student emotionally from the reading material and cause unnecessary stress—all of which can *lower* both comprehension and enjoyment.

Research tells us that good readers read at a faster pace than at-risk readers. It's also true that, compared to at-risk readers, good readers spend much more time reading and gain reading speed naturally. It does not necessarily follow that pushing at-risk readers to read faster and faster turns them into good readers. Faster reading rates can come about naturally. It's important to let the process of learning to read happen with as little stress as possible.

Jennifer Corn (2006) describes the extremely negative results of requiring her fourth-grade ESL students to read faster and faster. During their daily "fluency practice session," the students took word counts of their reading. Corn found that "the students who read the fastest were not consistently the best performers on other measures of reading" (p. 75). Corn also found that her students were nervous during their timed readings (exactly what we *don't* want for our children). As one of her students said, "I say, 'I'm gonna lose. I'm gonna lose. I better read faster,' and then I skip words or say the words wrong." Corn went on to say:

Explicitly teaching students to read quickly may have undermined their progress toward the underlying goal of fluency instruction—comprehension . . . The school did not reap many benefits from this focus on fluency. At the end of the 2004–5 school year, Gold Hills did not make adequate yearly progress in language arts. The school was closed, redesigned, and reopened. (p. 77)

OBTAIN PERMISSION FROM COPYRIGHT HOLDERS BEFORE RECORDING

You can record books, poems, and stories that are in the public domain, which means either that they were never copyrighted or that they were at one time, but are not copyrighted now. Works in the public domain can be recorded freely. To find out what works are in the public domain, visit these Web sites:

- http://www.pubdomain.com
- http://www.booksforabuck.com/general/pubsources/html
- http://www.authorama.com

You may also freely record materials if they are to be used exclusively by students who are blind or have severe visual impairments.

For works that are not in the public domain, *do not record them unless you have written permission to record from the copyright holder.* Be specific in your letter or e-mail to the copyright holder about what you want to record and the length of time you wish to use the recordings. Also, include in your letter your reason for audio-recording and who will use the recordings. A good resource on copyright law is your school librarian, as well as the book *Copyright for Schools* by Carol Simpson (2001). Simpson explains in detail the complexities of copyright for educators and the penalties for copyright infringement, stating:

The fair use analysis directs that the proposed copying or display should not adversely impact the market for or the value of the protected work . . . In simplest and most conservative terms, if the copying would deprive an author of a sale, the copying is not within fair use exemptions. (p. 15)

Teachers often believe that the fact that they are making print copies or audio-recordings of copyrighted materials for educational purposes protects them from any copyright violation or penalties. That is not true. In describing the liability of a teacher who makes copies of just a single workbook page for his or her students, Simpson warns:

The fact that a teacher or a school makes no financial gain on the transaction is secondary, as is the fact that one workbook page is a tiny fraction of the whole. The workbook is intended to be consumable; sales of multiple copies are supposed; hence circumventing this expectation is not appropriate use. (p. 16)

Lack of "appropriate use" can result in serious penalties. I highly recommend, therefore, the use of reading materials in the public domain, or obtaining written permission from the copyright holder. Permission needs to be granted in writing, and all such permissions should be carefully filed in a secure place.

FINAL RECOMMENDATIONS FOR TEACHERS

- Instruct each student in the proper care of and use of tape or CD players. Model the procedure for them, and then have them model for you. The extra time this takes in the beginning will be time well spent.
- Be sure to do the read-back portion of the method at least a few times per week. Include this in your lesson plans. It is most important to the success of the method.
- Remember that the choice and interest of the student are more important than the teacher's choice or preference, or any state mandates. At-risk readers in particular must be emotionally engaged in the reading material to make exceptional gains.
- Keep simple records of how the student is reading and how he or she is progressing. You might staple a list of the books or stories on one side of a folder, and on the other side of a folder staple a sheet with the date, book title, and comments. When listening to a student read, jot down notes describing the number of repetitions needed, quality of the student's read-back and summary, and the youngster's ability to answer a few comprehension questions.
- If volunteers or aides are conducting the read-back segment, be sure to train them in the record-keeping aspect. Also, be sure that you listen to each student yourself on a regular basis.
- For maximum results, students should work with the recordings at least four times weekly. At-risk readers should conference after each recording session. Good readers can conference every three or four readings.
- If read-backs pose a problem, divide the students into five groups. Each day, four groups can do an individual read-back to a peer or volunteer, with the teacher conducting read-backs with a different group each day of the week.

- Develop record keeping that allows you to track each student's progress. An "oral" portfolio is an excellent technique. Using a 60- or 90-minute audiocassette for each student, have the youngster record a self-selected paragraph on a regular basis. Before each recording, either you or the student should say the day's date. The students and their parents will be pleased to hear the improvement in oral reading over time.

Listen to Stories Recorded With the Carbo Method

Stories and books recorded with this method can be printed and heard, and are available for classroom use. See Appendix F for source information. These high-interest stories are recorded with introductions and endings for each segment, and in short amounts, using the correct pace and phrasing. Examples include recorded short stories, books, and comic books for Grades K–12, plus HI-LO (high-interest/low-readability for Grades 2–12) recorded stories for at-risk readers.

IN THE NEXT CHAPTER . . .

At-risk readers tend to be global, tactile, and kinesthetic. In Chapter 8, we'll look at ways to teach reading through high-interest materials that involve students tactilely and kinesthetically. This is another important resource that great teachers of reading use to reinforce their teaching skills.

8

Provide Opportunities for Active Learning

W e pass by a classroom, and there's lots of movement and activity. But are the students learning? While there's no doubt that active learning is important for many of our students, activity in itself may not help students to learn. Great teachers of reading understand the importance of active learning. They use it often instead of paper-and-pencil tasks, and they understand when and what kind of active learning should be used to help students advance in reading.

Brain research tells us that active learning enables students to process what they've learned on deeper, more lasting levels (Caine, Caine, McClintic, & Klimek, 2005; Sprenger, 1999, 2003). Remember, too, that many young children and at-risk readers are global, tactile, and kinesthetic learners who also tend to have high mobility needs.

Boys, in particular, are increasingly at risk in today's classrooms where students are often expected to sit still, listen, and fill out worksheets. Boys enter school less verbal and auditory and more tactile and kinesthetic than girls, and remain so throughout the grades (Thies, 1999/2000). Boys also consistently outnumber girls in remedial reading classes, are twice as likely to be identified as having learning disabilities and placed in special education classes, and by eighth grade are 1½ years behind girls in reading. It's no wonder that an increasing percentage of boys dislike school and do not attend college (Newkirk, 2003).

To teach reading skills well and to increase student motivation, it's important to accommodate the reading styles of students—especially boys—by cutting back on the use of worksheets and teacher lecture, and increasing the use of active learning (Dunn, Griggs, Olson, Gorman, & Beasley, 1995; Roberts, 1998/1999).

THREE LEVELS OF ACTIVE LEARNING

Let's look at simple ways to include *effective* active learning in the classroom. We'll move from the easiest to the more difficult methods to implement. In the next chapter on designing classroom environments, we'll explore ways of accommodating active learning through differentiated classroom design.

Level 1. Activity Separate From Learning

This lowest level provides some activity but is not necessarily related to the learning at hand. It helps to relieve the tedium that can be caused by sitting at a desk for most of the day. Movement serves to refresh youngsters physically and enables them to concentrate better on listening and on paper-and-pencil tasks. Children with high mobility needs feel great discomfort when they must sit for prolonged periods; that discomfort makes learning and concentrating difficult. As I noted in the opening portion of this chapter, this is especially true for boys.

The informal area depicted in Figure 8.1 provides a variety of comfortable seating arrangements that allow for many different learning activities, as well as for mobility. Figure 8.2 shows a standing work station that allows students to stand and move as they work. Standing work stations can be used for a wide variety of purposes, such as listening centers and game areas. Here are 10 successful techniques that teachers have used to give students a break from long periods of sitting. You can allow students to:

- Clean out their desks or parts of the classroom.
- Have jobs that allow some mobility (open/close windows, distribute/ collect papers, do errands).
- Sharpen their pencils, get a drink of water, or sign out to go to the bathroom.
- Stand at their desks while working, at least for some parts of the day.
- Move to a part of the room where supplies and worksheets are stored (instead of students sitting at their desks and waiting for paper to be passed to them).
- Move to centers to get needed materials.
- Go to the class library for a book.
- Sit in carpeted or pillowed areas to do their work.

Figure 8.1   This informal area allows differentiated learning and instruction to occur. Students can easily change their positions, shift to another place to work, work alone, or work together.

SOURCE: Photo by Barbara Hinds. Courtesy of Bob Hope Elementary School, San Antonio, TX.

- Stand in the back of the room to take notes. Provide clipboards so several students can do this at one time.
- Use a "thinking" area on the side of the room (perhaps a ledge near a window), so students can have a turn standing in this area and working. This provides a brief change in environment.

Level 2. Simulated Learning

A simulated experience often involves the students kinesthetically (whole-body movement), and usually requires small amounts of materials and preparation. These activities can be done with an entire class, but are more often appropriate for small groups. Most important, they enable the kinesthetic learner to learn and to express himself or herself through whole-body movement. Some examples of this kind of experience include:

- Students pantomime parts of a story or an answer to a question and then describe their answer orally or in writing.

Figure 8.2   Because many students sit for a good part of the day, standing work stations provide a chance for them to stretch their legs.

SOURCE: Photo courtesy of Featherstone Elementary School, Woodbridge, VA.

Figure 8.3   Standing and working at an overhead projector allows this student some mobility.

SOURCE: Photo courtesy of Roosevelt Elementary School, Medford, OR.

- On every bounce of a ball, a student spells the next letter of a word, or calls out a chemical symbol and its meaning, or recites a multiplication table. This activity can be done individually, or students can take turns within a group.
- Each student is given a "yes" card and a "no" card. Cards are held up to answer questions posed by the teacher or by another youngster. (This technique becomes self-checking when the students look at one another's answers.)
- A word is shown to a student, who pantomimes the word for another student or group to guess, or a word is stated and the entire class pantomimes the word.
- Two teams are formed. Items to be guessed have been placed on individual sheets of paper (e.g., book titles, explorers, compound words, verbs, names of states, and so on). Teams take turns selecting a paper. Within a time limit, one team member pantomimes what is written, while the rest of the team tries to guess what it is.
- Place a plain shower curtain on the floor; draw on it a computer keyboard with large keys. Pairs of students take turns spelling out a word by hopping onto the correct keys in the correct order.
- "Reading Jeopardy." Answers to reading questions are placed on cards. Two lines of students are formed, much like a spelling bee. Members of each team compete for points to provide the correct question for each answer.
- Half the students in the group write a compound word on a card and then cut it in half. The teacher mixes and distributes the halves. Then each child finds the classmate with the matching word half. Next, each pair of students acts out its word for the class to guess. This activity can also be used to match longer, multisyllabic words.
- Students role-play characters and events from a story, or they role-play an answer to a question.
- As a word is said, students clap once for each syllable. Variations: snap fingers, stamp feet, take steps.

Level 3. Games

During a long teacher lecture, it's painful to watch strongly tactile/kinesthetic students who are not auditory. They jiggle in their seats, fumble with pencils, doodle on paper, appear distracted, talk to their neighbors. Their behavior shows that either they're not on task or they're having a very difficult time staying on task. Watch these same students learning or reviewing the same content in small groups with games, and the scene is usually totally different. They're engaged, concentrating, having fun—and, most important, they're learning.

For tactile youngsters, learning that involves their hands helps them to learn reading skills faster. Here's why: When tactile students are touching game pieces, that tactile involvement creates a strong pathway through which learning can occur and be remembered.

Important note: In general, the use of the assisted reading methods should precede the use of games that practice reading skills. Students need to be able to read words fluently in context before those words and phrases are placed into a game format. Ideally, *after* youngsters can read a story fluently, then the words, sentences, and concepts can be practiced with hands-on materials.

Some examples of games include:

Small, Hands-on Games. Hands-on games can be used to teach specific reading skills. When starting, it's advisable to use a few standard formats and to cut and paste ideas from workbooks and other commercial sources. Appendix F provides source information for reading games and the learning materials listed in the following paragraphs.

- Task cards with matching parts are one of the simplest games to make. Figure 8.4 shows two types of task cards. For the book *The Littlest Rabbit,* by Robert Kraus, students sequence the pictures in chronological order and then match the correct sentence to each picture. The second set of task cards, using words from the topic The Human Body, requires students to match each word with its definition.

Figure 8.4

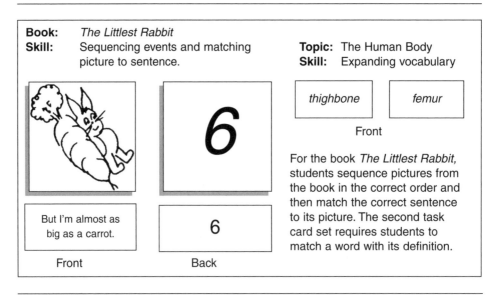

Book: *The Littlest Rabbit*	
Skill: Sequencing events and matching picture to sentence.	**Topic:** The Human Body
	Skill: Expanding vocabulary

thighbone   femur

Front

For the book *The Littlest Rabbit*, students sequence pictures from the book in the correct order and then match the correct sentence to its picture. The second task card set requires students to match a word with its definition.

But I'm almost as big as a carrot.

Front   Back

- A popular device enjoyed by students of all ages is the "flip chute" (Figure 8.5). The student places a card in the top slot of the flip chute with the answer on the reverse side of the card so it's not showing. As the card slides down the chute inside, it actually flips over and comes out the bottom slot with the answer face up, making the game a self-checking one. Students can play this game alone, with a buddy, or with a small group. Sample flip-chute cards are pictured in Figure 8.6.

- Pic-Wizard cards provide practice in developing a variety of skills, including: synonyms, antonyms, multiple-meaning words, and basic English. The student selects an answer by placing a pencil in the hole next to it, then checks to see if he or she is correct on the back of the card (Figure 8.7).
- The Power Reading Program has high-interest recorded short stories that are accompanied by reproducible games. See Figure 8.8.

Figure 8.5   These girls are making a set of vocabulary cards for their flip chute. One side of the card has an underlined vocabulary word in a sentence; the reverse side has the definition of the underlined word. When the card is placed in the flip chute, it flips over to reveal the answer.

SOURCE: Courtesy of Robb Elementary School, Uvalde, TX.

Figure 8.6   These flip chute cards help students practice comprehension and vocabulary skills.

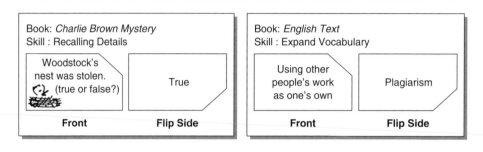

SOURCE: © National Reading Styles Institute, 1985.

Figure 8.7   These Pic-Wizard cards are easy to use and self-checking. The student selects an answer and turns the card over to check the answer.

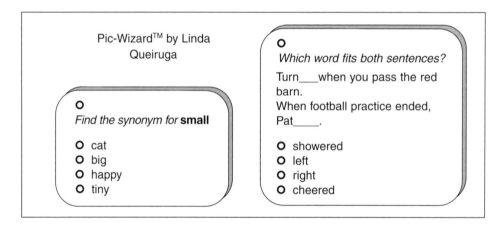

SOURCE: © 2001 Linda Queiruga, www.pic-wizard.com.

Figure 8.8   Power Reading Games

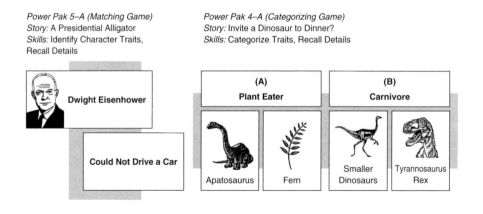

SOURCE: © National Reading Styles Institute, 2000.

Bulletin Board and Chalkboard Games. These games, which use the larger muscle groups, are excellent for kinesthetic learners. Simply make a large game and staple it to the bulletin board, e.g., large electroboards, pockets with cards to sort, and so on.

- In Figure 8.9 a young student "reads the room" by walking around the room and reading stories placed on the chalkboard.
- Figure 8.10 shows a girl matching a word card to a word written on the chalkboard and then tracing over the word.

Floor Games. Most games that can be placed on the floor allow students to use large muscle groups. These games are excellent for kinesthetic learners. Generally, teachers use shower curtains and other large pieces of plastic to create these games.

- Figure 8.11 pictures two young children playing a "scoot story" game. The story has been copied on construction paper, with illustrations made by the children. Then the handwritten pages of the story are laminated together. The children take turns scooting forward and reading aloud a page of the story, continuing until each has read the entire story.

Figure 8.9   While his teacher listens, a young student "reads the room" by walking around the room and reading the stories placed on the chalkboard.

SOURCE: Courtesy of Widen Elementary School, Austin, TX.

Figure 8.10   This girl matched word cards to words written on the chalkboard, and is tracing over one of the words.

SOURCE: Photo by Barbara Hinds. Courtesy of O'Connor Elementary School, Victoria, TX.

Figure 8.11   Two youngsters play the "scoot story" game. Each child takes a turn scooting forward one page of the story and reading the page aloud. This is an ideal activity for kinesthetic learners.

SOURCE: Courtesy of Roosevelt Elementary School, Medford, OR.

- The popular "word whacker" pictured in Figure 8.12 was created by drawing a keyboard on a sheet of plastic. Students "whack" letters with a fly swatter to spell out words.

Figure 8.12   Introducing the "word whacker." Forest Williams uses a fly swatter to spell out a word by "whacking" each letter in the word on the plastic keyboard.

SOURCE: Courtesy of West Amory Elementary School, Amory, MS.

- Finally, in Figure 8.13, two middle school boys are creating a sequencing game for their classmates to play. Once created, it will be checked, and they will then make the finished product.

Recommendations for Teachers

- Before the class begins work with a new activity or center, model and demonstrate the proper use of the activity. Ask for suggestions from students.
- Have the class assist in setting up guidelines for proper behavior. (They usually set much stricter guidelines than teachers would.)
- Move slowly when beginning activities and establishing new levels of student independence within your classroom. Establish, rehearse, and reward proper behaviors. Take time to explain the rules and discuss why they are needed.
- Students can assist in creating activities. Be prepared to accept game pieces and materials that are somewhat imperfect in appearance.

Figure 8.13   Ryan Neuhazen and Matt Mize create a game for their classmates to play. After it's checked, they'll make a final version.

SOURCE: Courtesy of Jim Hill Middle School, Minot, ND.

- Provide materials and clear directions so that older students and parents can help to create games.
- Work closely with the art teacher, the physical education teacher, and the computer lab technician (if your school has one). These subject-area teachers often can help to provide activities or game formats.

Remember that young children and underachievers tend to have strongly global, tactile, and kinesthetic reading styles. Active learning capitalizes on these styles and helps the brain to process information more completely and learn through multiple pathways. The resulting increase in student motivation and acceleration of learning are well worth the effort involved.

IN THE NEXT CHAPTER . . .

Chapter 9 will focus on designing classroom environments that enable great teachers of reading to differentiate their instruction in a wide variety of ways, including active learning and the use of brain research to guide a redesign of the classroom.

9

Design Student-Responsive Environments

In this chapter, we'll look at ways to design and organize classrooms so that they accommodate the reading styles of all students, *especially* at-risk readers. Let's review: We know that many young children and at-risk readers are global, tactile, and kinesthetic learners who have high needs for mobility and prefer to work in groups. When they read, they like soft light, informal seating, and choices of high-interest reading materials.

Unfortunately, most classrooms are not designed for the differentiated needs of students. Instead, they were designed to accommodate traditional teaching practices: teacher lecture, worksheets, and seatwork. However, brain research strongly suggests that the great majority of students do not learn most easily when they are inactive and quietly listening to a teacher lecture or when they are writing at their desks. Nor is learning enhanced when students work with reading materials that they find confusing and/or boring. Yet this kind of teaching persists. As Renata and Geoffrey Caine (1994) said, "One of the only places operating largely as it did more than 50 years ago would be the local school."

When changes are made that accommodate students' learning and reading styles, discipline problems diminish, and teaching becomes easier and more effective (Barber, Carbo, & Thomasson, 1998; Della Valle, 1984; Dunn et al., 1986; Krimsky, 1982; Pizzo, 1981; Shea, 1983). Great teachers of reading understand the whys and hows of designing student-responsive environments that motivate students to learn, provide for differentiated instruction, and greatly facilitate learning.

USE BRAIN RESEARCH TO GUIDE CLASSROOM REDESIGN

An important guide for designing effective, student-responsive environments is brain research (Caine, Caine, McClintic, & Klimek, 2005; Jensen, 1998a, 1998b; Sprenger, 1999, 2003). This impressive body of research tells us:

- *When the body is taken care of, the brain can turn its attention to other things.* It's important to accommodate the physical needs of all students, especially at-risk readers. Classrooms need some softly lit areas and places for students to work with small and large games (standing work stations, for example), as well as informal areas with soft chairs, rugs, and pillows.
- *The brain thrives on meaning. Information that is not meaningful will be lost.* All classrooms need high-interest reading materials that are modeled and recorded so that at-risk readers can read, understand, and enjoy them. Classrooms also need work stations, interest centers, and listening centers with a wide variety of well-organized reading materials.
- *The most powerful kind of memory is emotional memory.* Making classrooms warm, inviting, and attractive, with special places to read, helps the brain to associate reading with pleasure. Add to that mix high-interest reading materials that are sufficiently modeled for learning to occur, and the emotional memories are likely to be positive and lasting.
- *Multiple memory lanes help powerful learning to occur.* Students learn more easily when multiple senses are engaged, as they are with hands-on and kinesthetic activities.
- *Just the right amount of challenge or "stretch" encourages learning.* Many of our students have a reading level lower than their ability level. When traditional reading methods are used, these students are often given low-level reading materials, which bore and embarrass them as they struggle to read even those. These students benefit from high-interest, challenging reading materials and the modeling methods that will enable them to read those materials. Places are needed in classrooms where students can practice assisted reading methods together (e.g., echo reading, choral reading, paired reading), work in small groups, and work at listening centers with recorded stories and books.
- *Choice is important. It changes the chemistry of the brain.* Research in reading styles indicates that reading choices become increasingly important as students move up through the grades. Yet most older students rarely have the opportunity to choose what they read. For maximum reading progress to occur, classrooms need a wide variety

of reading materials based on students' interests, and places to store these materials so that they are easily accessible.

- *The brain is social. For most students, working together facilitates learning.* Places for group work are important. There should be both formal (upright chairs at desks) and informal areas (centers, soft furniture, pillows) that allow students to work together.
- *Positive emotions motivate and create excitement. Negative emotions dull the mind and create anger and fear.* Too often, students are taught with the wrong reading methods, forced to read materials they find dull, and continually overtested throughout the school year. The use of high-interest reading materials, reading games, and modeling methods, combined with inviting room environments, make students feel special, motivated, and excited about learning to read.

LET'S ADD WHAT WE KNOW FROM LEARNING STYLES AND READING STYLES RESEARCH

Figure 9.1 summarizes research studies that describe the learning characteristics of at-risk readers (Atchinson & Brown, 1988; Duhaney & Ewing, 1998; Dunn, Griggs, Olson, Gorman, & Beasley, 1995; Mohrmann, 1990; Sudzina, 1993; Thies, 1999/2000; Wilson, 1993). As you can see, as a group, these students have strong learning needs and preferences that do not match traditional classroom environments and the teaching that often occurs within

Figure 9.1   Environmental Accommodations for the At-Risk Reader

Typical Reading Style of At-Risk Readers	Environmental Accommodation
Global	Places for project work, high-interest materials
Tactile/Kinesthetic	Storage for games, spaces to play games on floor and at tables
High mobility needs	Informal areas, standing work stations, learning centers
Prefer soft light	Areas of soft light, lamps
Prefer informal design	Informal reading areas (e.g., pillows, carpet squares, soft chairs)
Unmotivated, prefer to choose what they read, need challenge	Wide variety of high-interest recorded materials, listening centers, tape players or CD players
Social, like to work in groups	Areas for group work
Need structure	Schedules, charts, routines posted

SOURCE: © National Reading Styles Institute, 2006.

them (formal seating, bright lights, standardized texts, teacher lecture, and extensive, independent seatwork).

Note: Many primary children and good readers also have reading styles that do not match this type of instruction. The classroom designs pictured in this chapter are beneficial for most students. Most important, research strongly indicates that when students' environmental preferences are met, they are more likely to associate reading with pleasure, read for longer periods, and, overall, achieve higher scores in reading (Della Valle, 1984; Dunn, Griggs, Olson, Gorman, & Beasley, 1995; Krimsky, 1982; Pizzo, 1981; Shea, 1983).

HOW TO IDENTIFY STUDENTS' ENVIRONMENTAL PREFERENCES

Have Students Draw Pictures

Some teachers begin the process of redesigning their classrooms by having their students draw pictures of themselves in an environment that would help them to read and to learn. Notice, for example, the different environmental preferences of Sarah and Mitchell (Figures 9.2 and 9.3).

It's obvious that Sarah likes QUIET! She also pictures herself reading in a formal position. Mitchell's drawing is quite different. His perfect reading

Figure 9.2   Sarah's drawing of her environmental preferences when reading indicates that she likes to read in a formal design and has a *very strong* preference for quiet.

SOURCE: Used with permission.

place is a soft couch near a lamp. Mitchell has even crossed out the over-head light to emphasize his dislike for bright light. (Note: For some young-sters, bright overhead lights can make the words shake and move on the page, give them headaches, and make them jittery. For more information on this topic, see Chapter 10 on reducing dyslexia).

It's easy to see that Sarah and Mitchell have very different environ-mental preferences. Multiply those needs times 25 or 30 students and you can see why it's important to redesign classrooms so that they can accom-modate a wide range of reading styles.

Use the Reading Style Inventory

A useful description of a student's or a group's environmental prefer-ences for reading is provided by the Reading Style Inventory® (RSI). If you recall, the RSI is an online questionnaire that provides Reading Style Profiles for individuals and groups. Looking at the first page of an RSI Group Summary Report, we learn the environmental needs of the students in this sixth-grade class (Figure 9.4). This particular group's strongest pref-erences for an environment in which to read indicate that they prefer little talking, or music, bright light, and some informal environments (such as reading in a soft chair or sitting on a rug or pillow on the floor). They are self- and adult-motivated and highly responsible; they prefer to choose what they read sometimes, read alone or with a peer (not unusual for sixth graders), have intake while reading sometimes (food and/or drink), read in the morning, and need little movement.

Teachers who work with the RSI generally start to redesign their class-rooms slowly. For example, for this sixth-grade class, a teacher might begin

Figure 9.3   Mitchell's drawing shows that he likes to read with soft light nearby, and to stretch out on something soft (like a couch). Notice that he *definitely* does not prefer overhead light.

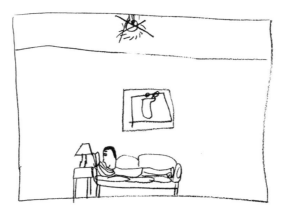

SOURCE: Used with permission.

Figure 9.4   RSI Group Summary Report

Group:	PAGE 1	Date: 10/11/06

Number of students in group: 25

Group/Analytic Tendencies

Minimal   Very strong
0 . . . . . 25 . . . . . 50 . . . . . 75 100

Global   *************************
Analytic   ***********************************

Perceptual Strengths/Preferences

Poor   Excellent
0 . . . . . 25 . . . . . 50 . . . . . 75 100

Auditory   ********************************
Visual   ****************************
Tactile   *************
Kinesthetic   *****************************

Preferred Reading Environment

Nonpreference   Strong preference
0 . . . . . 25 . . . . . 50 . . . . . 75 100

Quiet (no talk)   **
Quiet (no music)   ***
Bright Light   ******************************
Warm Temperatures *********************
Formal Design   ************************
Highly Organized   **

Emotional Profile. These students are

Not   Highly
0 . . . . . 25 . . . . . 50 . . . . . 75 100

Peer-motivated   ***************
Adult-motivated   *****************************
Self-motivated   ***
Persistent   **************************************
Responsible   **

These students prefer

Nonpreference   Strong preference
0 . . . . . 25 . . . . . 50 . . . . . 75 100

Choices   ************************
Direction   ***********************************
Work checked often **************************************

Sociological Preferences

Nonpreference   Strong preference
0 . . . . . 25 . . . . . 50 . . . . . 75 100

To read to a teacher   **************************
To read w/peer   ************************
To read alone   **
To read w/peer & teacher **************************
To read w/one peer   ******************************

Physical Preferences

Nonpreference   Strong preference
0 . . . . . 25 . . . . . 50 . . . . . 75 100

Intake while reading   ******************
To read in the morning   ********************************
To read in the early noon *********************
To read in the late noon **************************
To read in the evening   *********************************
Much mobility   **************

SOURCE: © National Reading Styles Institute, 1995.

NOTE: This RSI Group Summary describes an eighth-grade class's environmental preference while reading. Some of these preferences include quiet, soft light, and an informal environment. For a description of the Reading Style Inventory (RSI), see Appendix D.

by developing a small informal reading area with lamps and comfortable seating.

DESIGN CLASSROOMS THAT ENABLE HIGH LEVELS OF DIFFERENTIATED INSTRUCTION

A good classroom design facilitates the types of learning that will occur in that room. Figure 9.5 shows two small areas within a classroom that can be used by both individual students and small groups. The bookcase has been placed perpendicular to the wall and serves to divide the informal area and the listening center. The informal area has a beanbag and two pillows, while the tape players (or CD players) are permanently displayed at the listening center. Whether they are plugged into an outlet or operating on batteries, they allow students to sit down and immediately begin reading with their recordings.

In Figure 9.6 we see a traditional classroom in transition. There are desks for 24 students, plus two separated work areas—one informal and another that allows for group interaction. Instead of individual, separated desks, the desks are grouped together to create more space in the room. Note: Most teachers prefer low dividers so that they can easily see the students as they work.

Figure 9.5   Many teachers begin their room redesign by adding an informal reading area and a separate listening center.

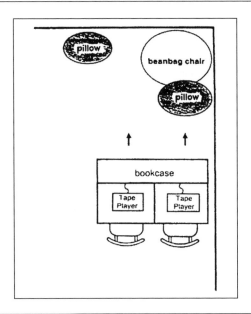

Figure 9.6   By grouping the students' desks, space is created for two separate areas in the back of the classroom.

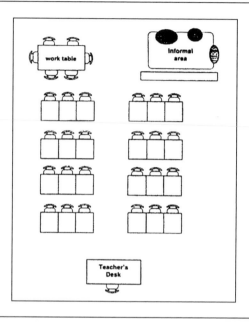

SOURCE: © National Reading Styles Institute, 1999.

Last, Figure 9.7 is an example of a classroom that allows for a great deal of differentiated instruction. It includes tables as well as desks, private and open places to work, formal and informal areas, learning centers, central storage of materials needed by the students (paper, pencils, markers, and so on) and a carpeted area with a stage that the students and the teacher use to present and put on small skits. Even the teacher's desk is used as a divider to save space. This classroom design allows for a great many differentiated activities, including small- and large-group instruction, student presentations, quiet working places, group work, informal areas, and work at learning centers. In addition, this type of design encourages independence (supplies are accessible to all), and requires a good deal of consistent, initial management.

Starting to Redesign a Classroom

Figure 9.8 describes eight ways to start redesigning a classroom. To gain space in your classroom, place desks together and, if you can, substitute a table for a few desks. The students who work at the table will need places to store their belongings in the classroom. Then begin your room design by adding an area (a listening center), a posted organizational device (charts, schedules), or different places for students to work (pillows, a rug). Provide the management needed. When enough time has passed and the change is running smoothly, try adding another area or procedure.

Figure 9.7   This redesigned classroom allows for large- and small-group activities, working alone, group work, and quiet and less quiet areas, and it provides both formal and informal areas. Note the "performing" and small-group area (carpet and stage) and the teacher's desk used as a divider.

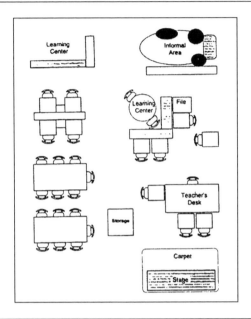

SOURCE: © National Reading Styles Institute, 1991.

Now let's look at some ways in which teachers have redesigned their classrooms. Figure 9.10 shows the use of a lamp to create soft light and a "homelike" feeling in the classroom. Figures 9.11 and 9.12 show ways to create informal reading areas, including "wandering pillows" that students can choose to take to their seats and use during reading time. Two quiet, private workplaces are pictured in Figures 9.13 and 9.14. In Figure 9.15, we see an ingenious idea for quieting down the noise made by chairs as students move them. This teacher likes quiet herself, so she cut slits in used tennis balls and had students place them on the bottom of their chair legs.

Listening centers are pictured in Figures 9.16 and 9.17. As you can see, tape players or CD players can be placed on tables, with headsets hung on hooks. The teacher who devised the portable listening center in Figure 9.17 has very little room, so several portable listening centers are stacked in a corner of the room; students can use them at their desks or in the informal reading area. The importance and use of listening centers is described in Chapter 7.

Figure 9.18 shows a place for small groups to meet, including a table in the classroom. Other elements of classroom design include an exceptionally peaceful reading area (Figure 9.19), a portable clipboard center (Figure 9.20), and a procedural sign (Figure 9.21).

Figure 9.8   Starting to Redesign a Classroom

Soft Light		Bring in lamps, loosen some overhead light bulbs, block light, sit near natural light, cover overhead lights with nonflammable acetate paper. (Make sure to check building codes with your principal.)
Informal Area		Place bookcase perpendicular to wall. Place pillows, rugs, beanbags on floor. Add couches, comfortable chairs.
Quiet Place		Use dividers to section off a small part of the classroom. Place a desk and chairs or pillows in the section.
Listening Center		Use formal or informal areas. Place listening center there. Have tape player plugged into the listening center.
Group Work		Can be done at a table, a desk, a low table (coffee table), or on the floor.
Interest Corner		Place all materials related to a theme in one place (books, filmstrips, games, recordings, etc.).
Schedules, Charts, Routines	GET TAPE / LISTEN / READ BACK	Place schedules and charts on walls and bulletin boards. Use large charts as dividers.
Storage		Store students' belongings in labeled cubbies. Also store manipulatives and art materials.

SOURCE: © National Reading Styles Institute, Inc., 1999.

Figure 9.9   Even the cafeteria is used for reading by students who love to read, like Shanesha.

SOURCE: Courtesy of Park Hills Elementary School, Spartanburg, SC.

Figure 9.10   Two students work together undisturbed in a separated area of their classroom. The soft light of the lamp adds to the feeling of informality.

SOURCE: Courtesy of Margil Elementary School, San Antonio, TX.

Figure 9.11   Seventh graders enjoy taking turns using these two "wandering pillows," which can be used at their desks during Continuum time.

SOURCE: Photo by Jill Haney. Courtesy of Mark Twain Middle School, San Antonio, TX.

Figure 9.12   A tub (available at Wal-Mart) provides a special reading place for these first graders.

SOURCE: Photo by Leighann Howell. Courtesy of West Amory Elementary School, Amory, MS.

Figure 9.13   Cardboard from a large box creates private work areas and a place to hang charts, work, or a headset.

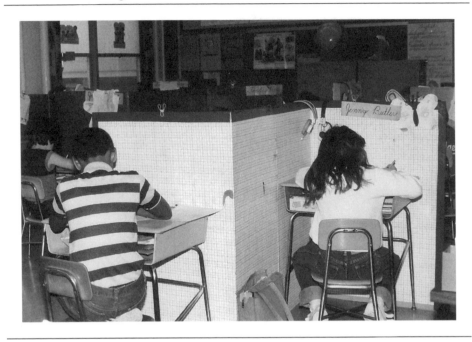

SOURCE: Photo by Mike Kasnick. Courtesy of the Butcher School, Emporia, KS.

Figure 9.14   A tent with pillows on the floor becomes a special place for reading.

SOURCE: Courtesy of Stemley Road Elementary School, Talladega, AL.

Figure 9.15   Placing discarded tennis balls on these chairs cuts down on the noise level (slits were made in the tennis balls).

Figure 9.16   The table and chairs serve as an ideal listening center. Tape players are plugged in and ready to use, with headsets hung nearby.

SOURCE: Courtesy of West Amory Elementary School, Amory, MS.

Figure 9.17   In this classroom, several portable listening centers are available. Since the tape players run on batteries, they can be used in any area of the room.

SOURCE: Courtesy of O'Connor Elementary School, Victoria, TX.

Figure 9.18   Three boys play a vocabulary game at this table. The boy on the left reads a vocabulary word, and the other two players have to find and read its definition.

SOURCE: Courtesy of Bob Hope Elementary School, San Antonio, TX.

Figure 9.19   With too few windows in her classroom, Barbara Hinds put up this peaceful mural in her reading area.

SOURCE: Photo by Barbara Hinds. Courtesy of Bob Hope Elementary School, San Antonio, TX.

Figure 9.20   Housing many clipboards in a crate creates a simple clipboard center. Students who need mobility while writing may take a clipboard and stand (or pace) in a specified part of the classroom.

SOURCE: Photo by Bonnie Bergstrom. Courtesy of Westridge Elementary School, West Des Moines, IA.

Figure 9.21   Here tape players are plugged in and ready to go, along with directions for using the equipment.

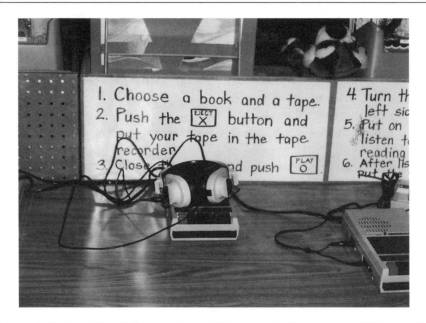

SOURCE: Photo by Jalma Fields. Courtesy of Dayton Public Schools, Dayton, OH.

Figure 9.22   Students will gravitate to their own special place to read, as has this young boy reading under a table.

SOURCE: Photo by Bonnie Bergstrom. Courtesy of Westridge Elementary School, West Des Moines, IA.

MANAGING THE PROCESS

Effective differentiated instruction requires varied working areas, materials, and procedures, as well as excellent management procedures and clear goals, such as:

- Create more independent and responsible learners.
- Enable students to learn from many sources, including teachers, peers, games, and so on.
- Build a "family" of learners who respect, protect, and care for one another.
- Allow students choices and movement so they can work through their strengths.
- Devise a structured system for checking students' work and check it frequently.

The primary goals for redesigning a classroom are to create an environment that allows for effective differentiated instruction, accommodates students' reading styles, and nurtures student independence. Here are some guidelines that have worked well in our model schools:

- Start slowly. Add one room area and provide the management necessary to make the change run smoothly.
- Empower students by teaching them about their styles. Teachers in our model schools explain reading styles to their students and meet with them individually to discuss their reading styles.
- Include students in planning the management at an appropriate level for their age. Discuss the guidelines or rules and, if necessary, the consequences if the guidelines are not followed.
- In the beginning, start with one center or area; rotate the class through it over a period of a few days. Set up a list of who goes when.
- When starting a new center, explain how the center works to the entire class, and then rehearse one group while classmates watch. For some classes, a few rehearsals may be necessary before the center is actually used.
- Establish a rule for how many students may work at a center. A common rule used by teachers is "four, no more." Depending on your class, the size of the group permitted to work together at a center can be reduced or enlarged.
- Decide whether you or someone else will assist a group at a center if they need help. The "someone else" might be a trained peer, an older student, or a volunteer.
- Plan and put into place what the other children in the class will be doing while you assist a group at a center.

- Have all materials ready in a center, equipment plugged in, written directions, and, especially important, *some form of accountability,* i.e., required written work placed in a basket in the center, a read-back of a recorded book, and so on.
- Assign one student in each group as the "technician" to work the equipment in a center.
- Post important schedules to serve as a visual reminder for students.
- If you move too fast in changing your environment and your students are not acting responsibly, pull back if needed by returning to more familiar, traditional ways of teaching. Then move ahead again more slowly.

Designing student-responsive environments helps students to concentrate and learn more easily and makes learning more enjoyable. Having said that, however, remember that it is the reading instruction that is most important. For example, if a student cannot hear sounds and has great difficulty learning phonics, providing the wrong work for that student in the form of many pages of phonics, while that youngster sits on a pillow next to a lamp, will just create a relaxed student who still has reading difficulties. The real purpose of good room design is to create more possibilities for excellent, differentiated instruction to occur. Those possibilities are more likely to become realities when reading instruction accommodates students' interests and strengths, and when good management procedures are in place.

IN THE NEXT CHAPTER . . .

We'll look at the important topic of dyslexia. Great teachers of reading know what it is, how it affects a student's reading, and how color can help to dramatically reduce the symptoms of dyslexia, i.e., moving letters, letters swirling, and lines of print "sliding" off the page.

10

Reduce Visual Dyslexia

Imagine that you are a student with visual dyslexia. When you look at a printed page, the words and letters reverse, swirl, and double. You rub your eyes and try again, but the letters are still moving. It's your turn to read and you know that you will struggle through, making many mistakes. Perhaps worst of all, you think everyone in your class sees exactly what you see on the page, and you can't understand how they can read so easily—and you can't.

WHAT DO THEY SEE?

When most of us look at black letters or numbers on white paper, we simply see letters, words, and numbers that don't move. It's what we've always seen, and it's hard to imagine anything different. Unfortunately, that's not what people who have visual dyslexia see. They report that letters and words on a page do strange things, such as reverse, double, shake, move up and down or sideways, slide off the page, appear and disappear. Colors may even appear and disappear—and more. As one boy with visual dyslexia said (putting it mildly), "It's just hard to read that way."

A vivid description of the extremely serious problems that can be experienced by people who have visual dyslexia is provided by Irlen (1991):

When words run like ants across the page, when the page changes color, when musical notes dance around on lines, when cars disappear and reappear next to you as you drive, when you play a sport and the ball isn't where it's supposed to be, when stairs look like a sheer slope, when you are not aware of how others perceive the printed page or what reading is like for them, then you don't understand why you can't do what everyone else can. (p. 3)

COLOR CAN HELP

Visual dyslexia is certainly not new. It is not a visual problem that can be helped with regular eyeglasses, and it affects people with a wide range of intellectual abilities, including those of great intelligence and talent. Most of us are familiar with the names of a few of the great and famous people who have had or have visual dyslexia, including Albert Einstein, Thomas Edison, Tom Cruise, Whoopi Goldberg, Robin Williams, George Washington, Cher, Pablo Picasso, Muhammad Ali, Walt Disney, and Danny Glover.

What *is* relatively new is the use of color—usually in the form of tinted eyeglasses and colored overlays—to reduce the symptoms of visual dyslexia. When the correct color is identified and used, many times the symptoms of visual dyslexia associated with reading can be reduced significantly. It's likely that many special education students and high school dropouts are youngsters with some degree of visual dyslexia that has gone unnoticed and untreated.

AN IMPORTANT DISCOVERY

In the early 1980s, a school psychologist named Helen Irlen interviewed 1,500 adults with reading problems. She identified a special subgroup with visual dyslexia who could decode words and had an adequate sight vocabulary but who reported a variety of visual distortions, found reading difficult, and avoided it whenever possible. Irlen also found that treatments from various professionals—optometrists, neurologists, psychologists, reading specialists, and so on—generally provided little or no help.

Irlen wanted to find treatments that would provide significant help for people struggling with visual dyslexia. She did, and it happened quite by accident one day as she was working with five students who had visual dyslexia. One of her students had brought in a red colored overlay that had been used in vision training exercises. Another student took the red overlay, placed it over a page in her book, and made a muffled scream. *The letters on the page had stopped moving!* The remaining students all tried the red overlay over a page of print, but it did not work for any of them.

Irlen began experimenting with a wide range of different colored gels. This is how she described her results in her book, *Reading by the Colors* (1991):

> Of thirty-seven people with visual perception problems in the study, thirty-one were helped by the colored sheets. (And they helped fifty-eight out of seventy people tested in my private practice.) For each individual helped, certain colors could make things better but other colors could make things worse. But for each person helped, there was one color that worked best. After everyone had determined and used their own optimal color, they reported they were able to read better and longer. (p. 22)

Irlen continued with her work, finally establishing a series of clinics that identify the most helpful color for their clients and create tinted eyeglasses. She also developed a cadre of trainers. In 1988, her work was reported on *60 Minutes.*

Research indicates that both the visual acuity and reading achievement of students with visual problems are improved with the use of colored filters (Adler & Atwood, 1987; Henson-Parker, 1997; O'Connor, Sofo, Kendall, & Olsen, 1990; Robinson & Conway, 1990).

SEEING WHAT THE STUDENT SEES

Helen Irlen's discovery of the effectiveness of colors was of great importance for people who have visual dyslexia. But the work of Dorothy Henson-Parker, building on Irlen's work, goes a critically important step further. Henson-Parker, a former school psychologist who has worked since 1975 with students with learning disabilities, developed many useful strategies, including the ground-breaking technique of taking copying samples that show what students who have visual dyslexia actually see (Figures 10.5 and 10.6). In my opinion, it is Henson-Parker's copying samples and her important assessment videos and manuals that provide the most helpful and practical strategies for teachers.

Particularly useful for educators are Henson-Parker's manuals and training videos in her *See It Right!* program (Henson-Parker, 2003a, 2003b; 2005). Actual student breakthroughs occur on the videos, such that while viewers are learning how to assess and use color and other strategies to help students who have visual dyslexia, they also experience the surprise and joy the students feel as the letters and words on the page stop moving. This emotional connection between viewer and student is made even stronger when the trainer on the video takes a student's copying sample. The dramatic difference between the two samples (without and then with the colored overlay) demonstrates what the student actually sees, and how the colored overlay improves the youngster's visual perception.

Figure 10.1   The dark pink overlay helps this girl see the print more clearly and read with greater ease.

SOURCE: Photo by Michael Flower. Courtesy of the National Reading Styles Institute.

Figure 10.2   The child with the sunglasses is light-sensitive and able to read for longer periods with the sunglasses on.

SOURCE: Photo by Mrs. Truesdell. Courtesy of West Amory Elementary School, Amory, MS.

Figure 10.3   This fourth grader reads with greater ease with a turquoise-colored overlay.

SOURCE: Photo courtesy of Robb Elementary School, Uvalde, TX.

Figure 10.4   Before using the pink overlay, Pernille reported that the lines twitched and she constantly lost her place on the page. With the overlay, she has no need to point at the words as she once did because all the print holds still.

SOURCE: Photo by Susanne Aabrandt. Courtesy of Rosalund School, Vaerloese, Denmark.

TWO STUDENT BREAKTHROUGHS

The breakthroughs of Brittany and Kevin are transcribed below from the *See It Right!* training videos. At this point, each child is at Step 3 in Henson-Parker's four-step assessment process.

Brittany: Color Testing. Brittany's color testing is in progress on the video, and her personal breakthough is about to happen. As the scene opens, the screener, Romy Sperling, a resource specialist from Los Angeles, is seated next to Brittany at a table. A storybook with words on each page lies open in front of Brittany. Mrs. Sperling places a light blue overlay over one of the pages. The page next to it has no overlay. Notice how self-aware Brittany is when she says that she knows "when they're gonna move" (the letters and words):

Mrs. Sperling: Is there any difference?

Brittany: It still does the same thing.

Mrs. Sperling: Okay. Hopefully one of them does something different.

(Mrs. Sperling replaces the light blue overlay with a yellow one. Then she gestures left to right above the two pages—one with and one without an overlay.)

Mrs. Sperling: Compare this page to this page.

Brittany: Still the same.

Mrs. Sperling: Same.

Brittany: It's kinda easy to tell 'cause I know when they're gonna move.

Mrs. Sperling: *(Replaces the yellow overlay with a purple overlay.)*

Brittany: Everything's holding still.

Mrs. Sperling: Is that good?

Brittany: *(Nods, shifts in her seat, and stares intently at the words under the purple overlay.)*

Mrs. Sperling: And now I'm still gonna try the other colors and see if we can make it even better, okay?

Brittany: Okay.

Mrs. Sperling: But I like that they're holding still.

Brittany: But they're almost . . . but they're trying to move . . . but this won't.

Mrs. Sperling: They're trying . . . okay.

At this point, it is later in the demonstration. A green overlay is over one page, and the purple overlay is over the opposite page.

Brittany: (*Takes the purple overlay off the page of print and hands it to Mrs. Sperling.*) This one's going up and down now.

Mrs. Sperling: (Replaces the purple overlay with a dark blue one.)

Brittany: Now that one won't let them move at all!

Mrs. Sperling: No?

Brittany: No!! (Decisively said.)

Kevin: Validating Results. The following conversation between Kevin and his teacher, Linda Powell, a National Board Certified Teacher from Whittier, California, reveals to us why Kevin has hated to read for a long time. When the conversation begins, Kevin (with a big smile) has just finished his first effortless reading of a passage. Note: Both Kevin and Brittany were helped by a dark blue overlay placed over the print. This was just coincidence.

Mrs. Powell: What do you think is the difference between using the blue color or not using it?

Kevin: It's harder reading.

Mrs. Powell: With or without the color?

Kevin: Without.

Mrs. Powell: Tell me how you feel when you're using the blue color.

Kevin: Not dizzy.

Mrs. Powell: Not dizzy? It makes you dizzy when you see the plain white page.

Kevin: Yeah.

Mrs. Powell: How do the words look when you're reading without the color, and then when you're reading with the color?

Kevin: Up and down.

Mrs. Powell: Up and down? Without the color they're up and down.

Kevin: Yeah.

Mrs. Powell: What do you mean "up and down"?

Kevin:	(*Gestures with his hands.*) They're going up and down, zig-zag.
Mrs. Powell:	They are? And then what happens when you put the color on top of the words?
Kevin:	They stay.
Mrs. Powell:	They do? So would you think that using color helps you?
Kevin:	Yeah.
Mrs. Powell:	Can you tell me how?
Kevin:	By not giving me a headache when I read just the white paper with black.
Mrs. Powell:	It gives you a headache?
Kevin:	Yeah, that's why I don't like reading.

IMPORTANCE OF TAKING COPYING SAMPLES

What I particularly like about Henson-Parker's work is its practicality. It's one thing to describe what students with dyslexia *seem to see*; it's quite another *to show what they actually do see* by taking copying samples. The student copying samples in Figures 10.5 and 10.6 help teachers and parents to understand the impact of the visual distortions these children experience every day, as well as the help provided by a colored overlay. What follows is Henson-Parker's analysis of these two copying samples.

Analysis of Two Copying Samples

Vera—Second Grade. In Figure 10.5, we see Vera's before and after copying samples. After identifying the dark green overlay as the one that helped Vera the most, copying samples were taken. Vera was asked to copy the words from a page in her book, exactly as she sees them—first without the dark green colored overlay, and then with it over the same page of print. Without the colored overlay, Vera's letters have extra marks on them, some are backwards (s, r, a, d, and e), and some are out of order or wrong. The "s" at the beginning of the second line is extra, and the "t" that follows is spaced far away from the "he" which would form the word "the." With the dark green overlay over the print, the letters have no extra marks, they are in the correct order, none are backwards, and there are no extra letters.

Vera's teacher reported that Vera was unable to sit still while reading, needed to use a marker, and read slowly and hesitantly. She also rubbed

Figure 10.5   Vera's Copying Sample

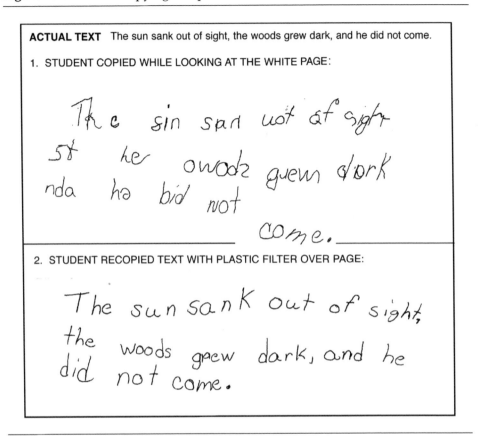

her eyes and held the page close to her, saying, "The white page is hard to see." When interviewed, Vera described what she saw without the use of color. This is what she said: "The beginning letter moves to the last letter and they switch places. Sometimes the whole word moves." When using color, Vera reported that "it looks real different. I don't see a lot of mistakes, a lot of ups and downs." Later, her teacher reported that Vera's oral reading was more accurate and noticeably faster when she used color.

Jimmy—Third Grade. Figure 10.6 contains Jimmy's before and after copying samples. The color that helped him was gray. Without the gray overlay, many of Jimmy's letters are backwards or upside down, and the word "coal" is misspelled. With the gray overlay, his letters are all correctly written and spaced well, and the word "coal" is correctly spelled.

After the color assessment, Jimmy said, "The words don't look scrambled. Without color, when I see the words, they're smaller. Lines get closer, and I could see some of 'em walk away [the letters]." With the color, Jimmy said, "The words stay where they are. They're not all crooked."

Figure 10.6   Jimmy's Copying Sample

ACTUAL TEXT COPIED: Mary dusted and ironed and brought in coal for the fire.

1. STUDENT COPIED WHILE LOOKING AT THE WHITE PAGE:

Mory dnsted ont !roued oud dronpht !u coo'
'Tor tde 'Ti re.

2. STUDENT RECOPIED TEXT WITH PLASTIC FILTER OVER PAGE:

Mary dusted and ironed and brought in coal
for the fire.

SOURCE: © D. Henson-Parker, 2005, www.seeitright.com.

How to Take a Copying Sample

After a color is identified that reduces or eliminates visual distortions for the student, the youngster is then asked to show exactly what he or she sees when looking at a page of print—first without color, and then with color. Henson-Parker recommends that the student begin this process by copying one line, or a few lines, of print from the page *without* a colored overlay over it. The copying is done on an unlined, plain white sheet of paper. It is here that we can see the visual distortions that the student sees. The student is asked to write or "draw" exactly how the letters, words, and spaces look to him or her when seen on the white page. Next, the student is asked to copy the same line or lines of print on another sheet of paper, with the colored overlay placed over the page of print. The very same directions are given to the student.

This is when we see how and to what degree the colored overlay corrects the letters and words for the student. This strategy enables educators, parents, and students *to actually see* the types of visual distortions that youngsters with serious visual perception problems experience, and how the use of color reduces those distortions.

SYMPTOMS AND RECOMMENDATIONS

The visual problems of students with visual dyslexia tend to cluster into two main categories: incorrect visual input and discomfort when looking at a page of print. This section is adapted from Henson-Parker's work.

Incorrect Visual Input

When a student has difficulty seeing the print on a page, it may be that he or she is receiving incorrect visual input. The student attempts to figure out what is on the page, and then tries hard to read it. This process can take some time because often the words, as they are perceived by the student, don't make much sense. When students don't perceive the print correctly, they see a poor visual model, and their copying reflects what they see. Teachers and parents are outside of this process; all they see is the student struggling hard to create meaning from what he or she sees.

Discomfort When Looking at a Page of Print

Black letters on a white page can cause problems for youngsters, especially when viewed under a bright light. For the student, the page may appear too bright, which may cause discomfort. What the student experiences may be caused by the sharp contrast of the black letters on a white page. Or it may be that the moving and changing letters, words, and spaces are so difficult for students to look at that they rub their eyes, look away from the page, put their head down, or interrupt their focus on the page in some other way. Note: When they do this and then look back at the page, often their eyes have had a rest and the print appears stable again.

To help you determine which students in your class might have visual perception problems, Figure 10.7 contains a listing of typical behaviors of students who are sensitive to light. When many of these symptoms are observed in a student about 6 years of age or older, classroom interventions can be tried (Figure 10.8). If these are not successful, the possibility that the youngster has visual dyslexia needs careful consideration. As a first step, of course, the student should be referred to the school nurse for both near- and far-point visual acuity screening, and referred further to a medical vision professional, if indicated.

You can help those students who do have a visual perception problem by making adjustments in your classroom environment, and by carefully selecting the kinds of materials you provide. Often, the perception problems of these youngsters are worsened by certain kinds of lighting in a classroom. Fluorescent lighting appears to produce the most problems, including moving letters, headaches, eye pain, and difficulty seeing information placed on the walls or chalkboard.

In particular, the stark contrast of black print on white paper can cause these students to experience visual distortions. A strategy that has been successful with some students is to use different colored paper to print assignments. Each student does his or her own "research" by experimenting with the various colors and reporting back to you which color is the most comfortable and produces the clearest letters. (This "best" color may be different than the overlay color they use.) The use of colored paper can make it easier for the student to read the print since letters, words, and numbers will be shifting and moving less or not at all. In addition, be wary of complex

Figure 10.7   Symptoms of Visual Perception Problems

READING	• Slow, hesitant oral reading.
	• Difficulty keeping place.
	• Appears to read words backwards or out of order.
	• Reads the same word twice or skips a word.
	• Difficulty answering comprehension questions.
SPELLING	• Reverses sequence of letters.
	• Leaves letters out when copying words on a list.
	• Spells words *almost* right. Similar letter substitutions.
MATH	• Inaccuracies in computation.
	• Backwards numbers.
	• Crooked columns of numbers.
	• Numbers that don't look grouped when they're supposed to be grouped.
WRITTEN WORK	• Work completed very slowly.
	• Too much, too little, irregular and/or no space between letters and/or words; uneven margins.
	• Writing is above or below the line, varies, or appears wavy.
	• Skips lines, leaves out letters or words.
	• Reversals.
BEHAVIOR	• Appears distractible. Only reads, or attends to paper-and-pencil tasks, for a short time before losing attention.
	• Difficulty keeping eyes on the page when trying to read.
	• Squints, blinks a lot, rubs eyes, shakes head.
	• Complains of eye pain and/or headaches.
	• Shades eyes and/or book in some way.

SOURCE: © D. Henson-Parker, 2006, www.seeitright.com.

Figure 10.8   Accommodating Students With Visual Perception Problems in the Classroom

---

Classroom Lighting

- **Reduce the light:** Change the student's seat to a darker area of room, facing away from windows. Allow caps or visors to cut glare.

- **Reduce the general lighting.** Turn off half the lights (especially fluorescents); shut lights during periods of bright natural light or close window coverings; add lamps to areas of the room.

Distance Viewing

- **Use darker-colored markers on white boards.** Light colors are difficult to see and may appear as blank spots (no yellow or other pastels). Write with clear, large print so the writing is easily seen, and reduce or lessen glare, if possible.

- **Make copies of board work on colored paper.** Use the color that helps the student.

Use Colored Paper

- **Create journals on pastel-colored paper.** The 8 ½" × 14" size folded works well. For those who need it, make lines darker than the faint blue lines in most journals.

- **Duplicate assignments on colored paper.** The color should help the student to feel a greater degree of comfort and increase print clarity.

Clarity of Reading Materials

- **Provide clear copies.** They should be printed in ink dark enough to be seen easily.

- **Use an easy-to-read typeface for classroom assignments.** Extra lines/serifs can move and be confusing.

- **Provide a printed spelling or vocabulary list.** A light-sensitive student may copy words incorrectly and then study those words.

- **Allow students to place their books in positions that reduce glare.** Book stands sometimes help.

- **Enlarge the print of the work given to students.** The larger the letters and the more space between the letters, the less distortions tend to occur.

- **Use small magnifying bars to more easily enlarge the print.**

SOURCE: © D. Henson-Parker, 2006, www.seeitright.com.

typefaces. Simple, clear, large letters usually work best. Figure 10.8 has more suggestions for accommodating the student with mild to severe visual perception problems.

Visual Dyslexia vs. Auditory Dyslexia

There are two distinct types of dyslexia: visual dyslexia and auditory dyslexia. Most people assume that the term "dyslexia" always means visual dyslexia, but it doesn't. It's particularly important when conducting or evaluating research to know which type of dyslexia is being discussed. People with auditory dyslexia have auditory perception problems that can manifest as: difficulty in recalling and/or associating letters with their sounds; distinguishing between and among similar sounds; recalling and blending sounds to form words; and recalling what they hear. On the other hand, people with visual dyslexia look at a page of print and may see letters, numbers, lines of print, and/or words reverse, double, shake, move up and down or sideways. slide off the page, or appear and disappear.

Perception problems occur on a continuum from slight to severe. Some students have both auditory and visual perception problems, some severe enough to classify them as having dyslexia in both areas. These youngsters find it very difficult to learn how to read. To prevent failure, these students need IEPs that take into account their weaknesses and strengths, and that recommend the most appropriate reading strategies. Note: The Reading Style Inventory provides this type of information.

WHAT CAUSES VISUAL DYSLEXIA: TWO THEORIES

This chapter has focused on the positive effects of using color with students who have visual perception problems, some severe enough to be considered visual dyslexia. We have looked at the early breakthroughs of Helen Irlen and the work of Dorothy Henson-Parker. In this section, we'll examine two different theories that explain why people with visual dyslexia see a page of print as they do.

Theory #1

In 1991, a prominent group of brain researchers from Harvard Medical School reported that studies of people with dyslexia, as well as autopsies of the brains of people who had dyslexia, indicated that a cause might be a failure of visual circuits in the brain to keep proper timing (Livingstone et al., 1991). Prior to this study, experimental psychologists in Australia and the United States reported that people with dyslexia performed poorly on tasks requiring rapid visual processing (Blakeslee, 1991).

In the 1991 Livingstone study of people with dyslexia, stimuli were pre-sented visually at high and low contrasts and at different speeds. At high contrast, participants performed normally; at low contrast, they had a greatly diminished response, suggesting a sluggish magnocellular system. (Note: Scientists have identified two visual pathways in the brain. Each pathway carries different types of information: the magnocellular pathway carries fast, low-contrast information, and the parvocellular pathway carries slow, high-contrast information). Additional support for the theory that dyslexia might be caused by irregularities in the magnocellular system came to light when Livingstone's group compared the brains of five people who had dyslexia with the brains of five people who did not have dyslexia. The study found that the brains of those with dyslexia had "abnormalities in the magnocellu-lar, but not the parvocellular, layers" (Livingstone et al., 1991, p. 7943).

The findings of the Livingstone study suggest that dyslexia might be caused by the improper timing of visual circuits in the brain, and lends theoretical support to the use of colored filters in treating dyslexia. Prior to this study, most scientists believed that dyslexia was purely a language problem. An easy-to-read version of the findings of the Livingstone study is available in an article by Blakeslee (1991).

Theory #2

In 1998, professors at Yale University reported on a study in which fMRI (functional magnetic resonance imaging) recorded the brain activity of adults with dyslexia as they unsuccessfully attempted to sound out nonsense sylla-bles. The study found that the fMRI scans of the subjects with dyslexia showed less blood flowing to the brain's language centers than the fMRI scans of control subjects who were able to sound out the nonsense syllables. The study's authors concluded from these results that all young children need early, intensive phonemics and phonics instruction to form and open the lan-guage centers in the brain that receive this information (Shaywitz, et al., 1998).

Gerald Coles (2000, 2001, 2004) has discussed at some length the prob-lems in the Shaywitz study. For example, the Shaywitz study was con-ducted with a group of adults who had dyslexia, ranging in age from 16 to 58, who could not decode nonsense syllables. We do not know in what way these adults were dyslexic since, "except for their IQ-score range, we are told nothing else about them" (Coles, 2000, p. 63). Regardless, Shaywitz and her colleagues recommended the teaching of phonemics and phonics (which did not occur in the study) to all people with dyslexia and to young children beginning to learn to read.

In reviewing the Shaywitz study and others like it, Hudson, High, and Al Otaiba (2007) went a step further, stating that it is highly likely that visual dyslexia may not even exist, and people with dyslexia are not helped by col-ored overlays or tinted eyeglasses.

In his review of the Shaywitz study in *Misreading Reading: The Bad Science That Hurts Children*, Coles (2000) concluded:

An advanced technology [fMRI] will never compensate for the flawed theories, methods, and data interpretations that form and inform this and similar research. Since there is more at stake here than mere scientific inquiry, and since an extraordinary technology is being used to make unwarranted claims about how children learn to read, it is the potential harm to children that is most serious. (p. 68)

CONCLUSION

Great teachers of reading understand that visual dyslexia is a complex problem, and they know how to use color to help lessen or eliminate the symptoms. Research does indicate that both visual acuity and reading achievement are improved with the use of colored filters for students with visual perception problems (Adler & Atwood, 1987; Henson-Parker, 1997; O'Connor, Sofo, Kendall, & Olsen, 1990; Robinson & Conway, 1990). The use of colored overlays and tinted eyeglasses has helped some of these individuals to see print more accurately. When an overlay helps, the improvement is instantaneous. Henson-Parker's copying samples make this improvement very clear. More research needs to be conducted, especially involving Henson-Parker's strategy of obtaining students' copying samples. Researchers can use this technique to identify the kinds of problems being experienced by subjects in a study. For more information, see the following Web sites: dyslexiacure.com, seeitright.com, irlen.com.

IN THE NEXT CHAPTER . . .

We'll look at how to apply the strategies discussed so far to accommodate students with special needs, including those with learning disabilities, attention-deficit hyperactivity disorder (ADHD), emotional disorders, and giftedness, as well as students who are English language learners.

11

Accommodate Students With Special Needs

Sweeping societal changes in the U.S. are making themselves felt in our schools, particularly in the increased numbers of special-needs students. Today's teachers see drug babies, babies born out of wedlock, a growing number of single-parent families, poor and abused youngsters, and children with limited experiences and abilities in English.

—Marie Carbo

I wrote those words 10 years ago (Carbo, 1997c). Sadly, little has changed. If anything, the problems I noted have worsened. Students with special needs still tend to be the youngsters who are least likely to be served well within traditional classroom structures. Some have difficulty processing information, some fidget and are highly distractible, some are brilliant and easily bored, some are learning to speak English, and others have emotions and past experiences that make learning difficult. Whether they have learning disabilities, ADHD, giftedness, emotional disturbances, or are learning English, these students need reading instruction that accommodates their strengths and interests, thereby giving them the best opportunity for success.

There is some evidence of a healthy, new focus on early intervention. The Individuals with Disabilities Education Improvement Act (IDEA) of 2004, for example, directs schools to try effective interventions prior to considering a referral to special education. The practice that is being encouraged is called Response to Intervention (RTI). With this model, schools don't have to wait until a student falls behind to begin a structured process of providing assistance. In fact, the new legislation allows school districts to use up to 15% of their federal special education dollars for "Early Intervening Services" *before a child fails,* which includes the use of effective alternative strategies, reading methods, and programs in the regular classroom.

EFFECTIVE INTERVENTION STRATEGIES

This book is all about improving developmental reading programs and using powerful intervention strategies *before* students fail. For example, students who have difficulty learning with one reading method often can learn to read easily with reading methods that accommodate their learning strengths and interests; students with visual dyslexia can be helped dramatically with colored overlays; children learning English as their second language can improve their English and reading with assisted reading methods and with special recordings; and youngsters with high mobility needs are helped with opportunities for movement, hands-on resources, and a variety of learning activities and places to work.

Figure 11.1　Many Ways to Demonstrate Learning

Make a travel poster	Write a song
Do a puppet show	Make a time line
Write a letter	Make a video tape
Develop and distribute a questionnaire	Make a list
Plan a journey	Create a slide show
Design and construct a new product	Produce a film
Create a model	Make a collage
Write and produce a play	Collect pictures
Keep a diary	Write an essay
Have a panel discussion	Make a Learning Center
Give a demonstration	Prepare and serve food
Create a slogan or bumper sticker	Design and make costumes
Make a game	Make a tape recording
Create a slide show	Write an autobiography
Hold a press conference	Develop a display
Write a book	Conduct an interview
Create a recipe	Write an essay
Draw a graph	Hold a press conference
Make a mobile	Make a dictionary
Create a musical instrument	Teach a lesson
Design needlework, latch hook	Pantomime

HOW TO ACCOMMODATE CHILDREN WITH SPECIAL NEEDS

More than ever before, teachers need to be able to recognize and understand the reading styles of each child. They need a wide variety of strategies; they need to know when and how to adapt instruction to their students' needs; and they need adequate staff development, modeling, and coaching so that they become confident in fitting the most effective strategies for particular students.

General Recommendations for Teachers

- For all students, focus on reading comprehension and enjoyment. Use reading materials that interest and challenge children. Eliminate boring or inappropriate worksheets and stories.
- Learn a variety of reading methods so that you are able to adapt your instruction as necessary.
- Identify students' strengths and appropriate teaching strategies with the Reading Style Inventory®.
- Accommodate your students' needs during instruction. For example, plan for mobility, healthful snacks, music, and the use of colored overlays. If necessary, submit a request to the appropriate testing personnel for permission to use these accommodations during testing.
- Accommodate students' mobility needs with informal reading areas and centers in your classroom.
- Use peer tutors and volunteers. As appropriate, encourage students with special needs to tutor other students. Encourage cross-age and cross-grade tutoring. Organize parents and other volunteers to help.
- Allow youngsters to demonstrate what they have learned in a variety of ways.
- Touching and experiencing are important for many children with special needs. Teach with games often and include activities that provide large-muscle movement (drama, pantomime, floor games).
- Inform parents by letter of the different activities and behaviors they are likely to see in your classroom.
- Keep a running list of breakthroughs for students. Continually analyze patterns to determine what occurred and why.
- Set aside time to share your successes and problems with other teachers.
- Be a resource. Stay current with research and be aware of a variety of instructional strategies.
- Share articles related to the concepts and strategies in this book. Encourage other teachers to do the same.
- Order and use needed materials and equipment, card readers, typewriters, computers, specially recorded short stories and books, tape recorders, CD players, high-interest books, and games.

Figure 11.2   School volunteer Mrs. Wilma Andrews assists Ricky Watts as he reads a story to her.

SOURCE: Courtesy of Silk Hope Elementary School, Chatham County, NC.

ACCOMMODATING STUDENTS WITH LEARNING DISABILITIES

Youngsters with learning disabilities are often underachievers who have difficulty receiving, sorting, processing, comprehending, and/or producing information. The primary cause of these difficulties is neither an emotional problem nor a lack of language or intelligence. In fact, youngsters with learning disabilities may be exceptionally bright but unable to read simple words or recall math facts. Some brilliant people have had learning disabilities, including Albert Einstein, Nelson Rockefeller, and Thomas Edison. To succeed, students with learning disabilities must learn through their strongest modalities. These children often have dramatic perceptual strengths and weaknesses. Some are strongly visual but not auditory; for others, the reverse is true. And some have neither visual nor auditory strengths.

A child with a learning disability may receive distorted information, such as reversed letters (Henson-Parker, 1997; Irlen, 1991). He or she may have expressive problems; the youngster might receive information accurately but have difficulty demonstrating or expressing it—even though the information has been correctly received and understood. Since many of these youngsters experience repeated failure, they may be greatly stressed, unmotivated, and/or afraid to try.

Figure 11.3   After one year of working with recorded short stories in Linda
Queiruga's Reading Lab, Tony, a tenth-grade student with a
learning disability, made great improvements in speech and a
two-year gain in reading.

SOURCE: Photo by Linda Queiruga. Courtesy of Canyon del Oro High School, Tucson, AZ.

Recommendations

- For students with weak visual skills, place various colored overlays on
  a page of print. Allow students to use a particular color that is beneficial. The overlays can help many children process words and numbers
  more accurately. Use colored writing paper for students helped by this
  strategy.
- If a student has visual problems, try the Fernald Reading Method
  (Fernald, 1943). Using a crayon, write a word the child needs on a
  5" × 8" card. Have the child trace over the word a few times with the
  index finger of his or her writing hand while saying the word. Then
  the youngster writes the word into a story.
- For youngsters with reversal problems, experiment with enlarged,
  simple print. In math, make numbers large and place few examples
  on a page.

- Provide students with their own copy of needed information if they have difficulty copying from the board.
- Deemphasize phonics for students with auditory problems (Carbo, 1987).
- Try the following with youngsters experiencing memory problems: the Carbo Recorded-Book® Method (provides repetition of words within a high-interest story) and *Sight Words That Stick*® (teaches words with cartoon-like pictures and stories).
- Provide high levels of structure as needed. Post daily schedules and directions; discuss short- and long-term goals with students; organize materials; post clear, simple directions.
- Draw simple pictures to convey directions for students who cannot read well.
- For youngsters with handwriting difficulties, provide paper with larger spaces between lines, have them dictate their stories, and/or encourage them to use a computer or typewriter.
- Try turning notebook paper to the side so that the writing lines are vertical. Have students use these columns when doing computation to help keep the numbers lined up.
- Use paper with raised lines for students who have difficulty staying on the line as they write.
- Share your ideas for new floor games, manipulatives, etc., at faculty meetings.

Figure 11.4   This young girl listens to a Carbo tape as she reads a page of a story. She will move on to each page until the story is finished. (Each page of the story has been placed in a pocket on this large laminated sheet.) This activity engages four modalities: tactile (touching the words), kinesthetic (moving to each page), listening to the tape, and seeing the words.

SOURCE: Photo courtesy of West Amory Elementary School, Amory, MS.

Figure 11.5   Copying a word in a salt tray helps this tactile learner to remember the word.

SOURCE: Courtesy of Anthon Elementary School, Uvalde, TX.

Figure 11.6   Hearing the rhythm and pace of the Carbo recording helps this high school student with a hearing impairment improve her reading comprehension.

SOURCE: Photo by Linda Queiruga. Courtesy of Canyon del Oro High School, Tucson, AZ.

ACCOMMODATING STUDENTS WITH ADHD

The child with ADHD uses motion to bring his or her central nervous system to a normal state of arousal or alertness (Barkley, 1990; Flick, 1996; Hannaford, 1995; Rief, 1993; Wunderlich, 1988). Most students have little or no difficulty staying alert when they are still, but this is not true for the child with ADHD. These youngsters must move to stay alert—squirming, doodling, and wiggling. They are easily spotted in a classroom because their hands are often in constant motion, tearing paper, tapping pencils, and touching everything around them. They often are unaware of their own constant motion.

Understandably, children with ADHD find it difficult to attend to classroom instruction or stay on task. Too much information places them in a state of overload, causing them to withdraw or "tune out." They also tend to have weak organizational skills. Their lockers and desks may be extremely messy, and they may lose their homework and forget to do assignments.

What kind of instruction do these children need? Let's look at the child with ADHD in terms of his or her reading style strengths. Children with ADHD have an exaggerated reading style. They are extremely tactile and kinesthetic. To function well in school, they need extremely high-interest reading materials, sufficient modeling with assisted reading methods, a great deal of academically focused movement as they learn, brief assignments, assistance as needed during small-group and independent work, and some calming experiences during the school day. Recent research indicates that a few hours each day of intensive exercise, outside of or during school, may help students with ADHD to focus in their classes and eliminate or lessen the need for medication (Szabo, 2006).

ADHD is a medical condition that can be difficult to diagnose. Most children with ADHD are boys, who generally start school being less verbal than girls and remain more tactile and kinesthetic than girls throughout their school careers. As with children who do not have ADHD, some with ADHD are bright while others are not. Although the American Psychological Association has developed detailed criteria for identifying ADHD, children with emotional difficulties can sometimes exhibit similar symptoms, as can highly tactile/kinesthetic youngsters who do not have ADHD.

The entire reading styles philosophy works for these students because it meets their sensory needs naturally. For purposes of instructional planning, regardless of whether the term ADHD is used, youngsters who need to move in order to learn should have motion designed into their instruction. They need to walk, touch, and play while they learn during as much of the school day as possible.

Figure 11.7   The use of a therapy ball instead of a chair provides the constant movement this youngster with ADHD needs to perform his best. When his classmates line up, he just moves the ball near his desk and lines up with them.

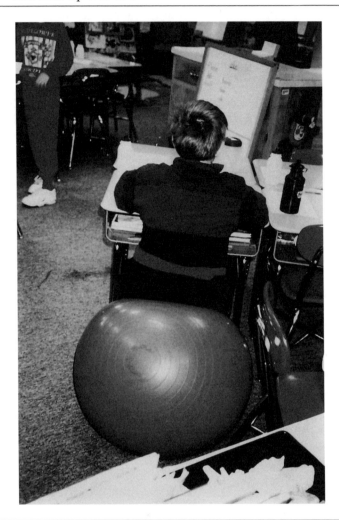

SOURCE: Courtesy of Silk Hope Elementary School, Chatham, NC.

Recommendations for Teachers

- Understand and accommodate the Reading Style of the tactile, kinesthetic, global child. In an exaggerated form, this tends to be the typical Reading Style pattern of the youngster with ADHD.
- Use a large variety of activities that accommodate the tactile/kinesthetic student, such as games, manipulatives, drama, and artwork.

- Accumulate files of effective manipulative materials and ideas. Share them with parents and staff.
- Tactile input stimulates the nervous system of the child with ADHD and usually improves concentration. Have "fidgets" available for youngsters who need them, such as squeeze balls, mini-puzzles, or rubber animals.
- Design a variety of instructional areas within your classrooms that allow children to move, such as informal reading areas, floor work, board work, and small-group work.
- Work with your art and physical education teachers to create classroom projects that involve children's large and small muscles as they learn.
- Teach with centers. If you have not employed this strategy, begin with one center that contains directions, objectives, and a variety of ways to learn and demonstrate mastery of information. You might include any or all of these elements: games, recordings, arts and crafts, worksheets.
- Try alternative seating that allows the child with ADHD increased movement, such as therapy balls, T-stools, or, if the condition is not severe, soft furniture that allows the youngster to shift position easily.
- Provide brief assignments that are somewhat challenging but not frustrating. Check the youngster's work often and praise as appropriate.
- Provide help in organization by color-coding subjects, verifying that homework is written down and completed, giving clear directions, and scheduling quiet times for checking work.
- Try allowing students to work in pairs and in small groups to help keep the child with ADHD on task.
- Provide experiences that help to calm the child with ADHD, such as soft light, music, snacks, and soft furniture. Several research studies have recommended Baroque music.
- Try raps or songs containing words or information you want students to remember.

ACCOMMODATING GIFTED STUDENTS

Gifted children are often underserved and misunderstood in our schools. Budget cutbacks have limited services in many locales to pullout programs for the academically and creatively gifted. Initially, gifted youngsters were identified based on IQ scores alone; now, however, rating scales and test scores are used in addition to or in place of the single IQ score.

Many states are serving gifted students in regular classrooms. At times, gifted youngsters are being pulled out for specific projects or areas of study. The resource room concept is being used less and less, and classroom teachers are expected to accommodate gifted youngsters through curriculum compacting, projects, and a more individualized approach to teaching. The teacher of gifted students is becoming a resource to classroom teachers, helping them to locate materials and design areas of study. Classroom teachers are also encouraged to identify those students who are not classified as gifted but who exhibit gifted behaviors, and to include those children in projects or areas of interest.

Sometimes gifted children have difficulty learning to read. More often, they read well but may become bored and unmotivated by a school's reading program. An understanding of the reading styles of gifted youngsters is critically important.

Gifted children have many different reading styles. When administered the Reading Style Inventory, gifted youngsters often, but not always, score highly across all perceptual areas. Many of these children do not prefer lectures because the pace of most lectures in the regular classroom moves too slowly for them. They do enjoy lectures that challenge their minds; they may also prefer self-paced activities such as teaching games, challenging software, projects, independent study, and peer teaching (Ford, 1996; Renzulli, 1994; Walker, 1994; Winebrenner, 1992).

Not all gifted students are teacher-pleasers, nor do they necessarily complete paper-and-pencil work in a timely manner. They often like choices that include their own suggestions.

Recommendations for Teachers

- Attend trainings for classroom teachers on strategies that accommodate the above-level reader.
- Add to your classroom library reading materials that are well above grade level across a wide variety of subjects.
- Place greater importance on stimulating high-level thinking skills and knowledge, rather than on neatness and punctuality alone.
- If your school employs a pullout program for gifted students, support and enforce a policy that does not require gifted children to make up the work missed when they are not in their regular classroom.
- Be flexible. Your gifted students may not need to be in the regular, on-grade-level reading program. Experiment with allowing gifted readers to read books of their choice.
- Remember that high-performing readers may still have difficulty with certain reading skills. If a youngster reads well without these skills or is unable to master them, do not teach the skills.
- Give many choices for both book selection and book projects.
- Although gifted students often need the socialization provided by cooperative reading groups, plan times when gifted youngsters can choose to work alone or with other gifted students.
- Remember that the gifted student is not an assistant teacher. Some enjoy assisting other students; some don't. Provide opportunities for them to work with other bright students or to work alone.

- Don't compare the work of less-capable students to the work of the gifted child. Such comparisons can be a source of embarrassment to both.
- Try curriculum compacting for students who quickly grasp new material.
- Initiate a research project.
- Encourage use of technology to expand a subject area.
- Allow students to find information using the Internet.

ACCOMMODATING BILINGUAL/LEP STUDENTS

Bilingual/LEP (Limited English Proficient) students can find it difficult both intellectually and emotionally to learn a new language. These youngsters come to school with varying degrees of proficiency both in their native language and in English. Some bilingual youngsters are proficient in both, some in one language, and some in neither language. Those who are limited in English often feel shy and embarrassed in American classrooms.

Schools need to provide risk-free, comfortable, relaxing environments where language and academic abilities can develop naturally. Possible environmental accommodations are soft music, snacks, soft light, comfortable furniture, and learning centers.

The first key to accelerating learning is knowing and understanding the bilingual youngster's Reading Style. The style of the bilingual/LEP student may vary greatly, depending on the individual and the cultural impact of his or her heritage. These youngsters learn more easily if the material is highly meaningful to them. Activities that expand upon and activate a youngster's prior knowledge are also likely to accelerate learning.

Reading methods that have worked extremely well with bilingual youngsters are the Language-Experience Method and the assisted reading methods. These are global reading approaches that enable youngsters to develop language and reading abilities with high-interest, confidence-building activities.

The instructional recommendations that follow can be used with both ESL programs (English only) and bilingual programs (using both English and the student's native language). The strategies recommended—recording books, active learning, story writing, and so on—have been highly effective with bilingual/LEP youngsters regardless of the type of program in which they participate (Gibbons, 1991; Spangenberg-Urbschat & Pritchard, 1994).

Recommendations for Teachers

- Learn expressions in the native language(s) of your students. Use the expressions to help them feel accepted.
- Provide print-rich environments in English and, when feasible, in the students' native language(s).

- Use many small-group, interactive strategies, such as cooperative and collaborative learning.
- Stock your class library with books in English and in the native language(s) of your students.
- Use many hands-on activities, projects, and product creations.
- Use a meaning-centered curriculum to aid learning and language development.
- Gear instruction at or slightly above the students' level of language proficiency.
- Try the language-experience method to teach reading and writing. This approach allows students to dictate or write interesting, simple stories and then use choral reading or paired reading for additional practice.
- Display lots of children's writing. Encourage the development of books written by children. Laminate them, record them, and store them in your classroom for student use.
- Record books, magazine articles, and short stories using the Carbo Recording Method. This method enables students to hear and see the structure of the language they are learning. Both vocabulary and understanding build quickly due to the slow pace, the small amounts of written material recorded on a tape side, and the repetition allowed. (Before recording, obtain written permission to record from copyright holders.)
- When necessary, record the introduction to a story in the youngster's native language. Then record the story in English.
- Allocate ample time for students to listen to taped passages while they follow along with their finger in the text. Make certain to provide time for youngsters to read back to more proficient readers (teacher, volunteers, peers).
- Allow students to take home and use recorded materials.
- Obtain written permission from the copyright holders of your textbooks. Then record textbooks at a regular pace and make them available for students.
- Hold schoolwide fairs and other special events that highlight and share native foods and language, and information about culture-specific events.
- Hold parent trainings on reading styles and the Continuum of Assisted Reading Methods.

ACCOMMODATING STUDENTS WITH EMOTIONAL AND BEHAVIORAL DISORDERS

Students with emotional challenges are often targeted for special services when their behavioral patterns make learning difficult for themselves and for their classmates. Identification of special services for these students should be done after specially designed educational support services and intervention strategies have been tried in the regular classroom and a youngster still exhibits patterns of inappropriate behavior.

Such behavior may make adequate academic progress difficult even though the youngster does not have a learning disability. Under normal conditions, the child might exhibit inappropriate or immature types of behavior or feelings. The child may suffer from pervasive unhappiness or depression, or may have a tendency to develop physical symptoms, such as severe pains or fears associated with personal or school problems.

Whatever their origin, students' emotional difficulties can interfere strongly with learning. The needs of these students can be quite complex. The move toward inclusion may mean that these youngsters receive their academic instruction in a regular classroom with supportive services provided, or in an alternate setting.

Since the challenging condition varies from child to child, there is no dominant perceptual strength. Youngsters with emotional challenges can display a wide range of cognitive abilities. Accommodating the interests and strengths of these youngsters provides the foundation for success. A great many activities taught in the reading styles approach target their needs. Generally, children with emotional challenges profit from instructional methodologies that reduce frustration and stress.

Recommendations for Teachers

- Create a team-developed individual educational plan (IEP). In addition to key staff members and parents or guardians, try to include the input of others who have a good relationship with the child (the custodian, the cook, a friend, etc.).
- Develop a variety of hands-on materials, such as self-checking task cards, flip chutes, and electroboards. These devices can be individualized while allowing the child some control.
- Graphically chart the child's positive behaviors. These charts should be private so that each child competes only with himself or herself.
- Reduce the causes of disruptive behavior. Find and support activities that provide positive reinforcement on the academic level of the student.
- Develop activities that provide the student with acceptable choices. For example, the child may choose the order in which to complete tasks, or may be given a choice of two out of three tasks to complete.
- Use the Carbo Recording Method with students who need to improve their reading. This method offers an escape from classroom distractions while enhancing the child's reading ability. In addition to focusing the child and increasing reading fluency, the read-back provides one-on-one time with the teacher.
- Challenge but try not to frustrate the children. Use self-checking materials, games, and brief assignments.

- Reduce feelings of failure and low self-worth. When grading papers, try placing checkmarks on all the correct answers. Allow the child a chance to correct those that are wrong, or work with him or her to correct them.

IN CONCLUSION

Each youngster brings unique strengths and experiences to school that deserve to be recognized and nurtured. Business as usual in American schools—textbook-dominated instruction, short-answer evaluations, and lecture-dominated teaching—seldom works for our children with special needs. Great teachers of reading provide these youngsters with a wide variety of strategies and materials that accommodate their interests, strengths, and needs.

IN THE NEXT CHAPTER . . .

We'll look at the ticklish topic of testing—how to prepare students for the inevitable tests in ways that are educationally sound, and that accommodate their reading styles. Chapter 12 is full of tips about preparing your students to do well on reading tests *without* taking an inordinate amount of teaching time, and special strategies to use as testing time approaches.

12

Prepare Students for Tests

Y ou are well on your way to becoming a great teacher of reading. Your students have shown dramatic improvement in reading this school year. They have become *readers!* They're reading much more difficult books than they did at the beginning of the year, and with good fluency and comprehension. They enjoy reading, check out many more books from the library, read voluntarily during some free moments in class, talk more about their favorite books—and some of them even take books to the cafeteria to read at lunchtime! Unfortunately, as things stand today, those extremely important measures of reading success go largely unnoticed. What counts are test scores.

One of the problems created by today's enormous overemphasis on test scores is the amount of time taken during the school day to prepare for year-end tests. In many schools, tests drive instruction. Too often, test preparation steals time from the kind of reading instruction and reading practice that at-risk readers need to become motivated, successful readers. When an inordinate amount of time is spent practicing for tests, scores may increase slightly, but the very large gains that could be made are lost. Large amounts of test practice can create undue stress and boredom, reduce voluntary reading, and leave too little time for the use of powerful reading strategies that can raise students' reading levels quickly.

TEST PREPARATION SHOULD BE EDUCATIONALLY SOUND

With reading ranked as the top educational priority, our students do need to learn how to perform well on reading tests. But it's important that test preparation be brief, fun (if at all possible), and *educationally sound*. In this chapter I will discuss how to:

- Increase voluntary reading
- Accommodate students' reading styles
- Identify reading objectives
- Determine which objectives to teach
- Practice sample items
- Teach test-taking strategies
- Prepare students as testing time nears

INCREASING VOLUNTARY READING

To perform their best on reading tests, students need to spend most of their reading time listening to, reading, sharing, enjoying, and discussing stories and books—not preparing for reading tests. The more time students spend reading voluntarily because they genuinely want to, the better they will perform on reading tests (Allington, 2001; Anderson, 1996; Krashen, 1993).

Research on voluntary reading sends a strong message to educators. Throughout the school year, at-risk readers need positive, enjoyable, and fail-safe experiences when they read. They need to spend plenty of time hearing good reading modeled, as well as practicing their reading with the aid of modeling methods. The more at-risk readers become comfortable and familiar with the sound and feel of well-written language, the more likely they are to improve in their reading and perform well on reading tests.

Research also tells us that only small amounts of time should be spent using worksheets that resemble the test. This practice is especially effective in small, regular amounts a few months before the test. An overuse of worksheets often creates stress, boredom, and a dislike of reading and *reduces* voluntary reading. Throughout the years, the National Assessment of Educational Progress (NAEP) has recommended a sharp decrease in the use of worksheets to improve students' reading abilities.

WHY IT'S IMPORTANT TO ACCOMMODATE STUDENTS' READING STYLES

Many at-risk readers are taught and tested through their reading style weaknesses. When this happens, learning to read becomes extremely difficult and stressful. We know that when we accommodate students' reading style

Figure 12.1   Improving Test Scores With Reading Style Strategies

---

- **Provide colored overlays for students who need them**. As discussed in Chapter 10, colored overlays can be the quickest way to improve a student's reading achievement. When a youngster is having trouble actually seeing the words correctly and a colored overlay is found that steadies the words on the page, there is usually instant improvement in reading. Students who benefit from using colored overlays should be permitted to use them when they take tests.

- **Use Carbo recordings.** During the school year, at-risk students should use high-interest, challenging reading materials recorded with the Carbo method at least four times weekly. Research strongly indicates that this practice will improve their fluency, comprehension, and vocabulary achievement.

- **Use many tactile and kinesthetic materials to practice skills**. By creating gamelike skill practice that students can play together and discuss, stress is decreased, and your tactile and kinesthetic learners will learn and recall the skills better.

- **Try to schedule the test at the best time of day**. Students have energy highs and lows. If you can, schedule your testing time during the period when student energy is high. For many at-risk readers, that time is late morning. Ask your students when they feel they would perform best on a test.

- **Allow students healthful snacks**. Snacking can increase energy and reduce stress. Rehearse procedures for snacks and establish definite rules before the testing dates. Some appropriate snacks are raisins, carrots, dry fruit, popcorn, and celery sticks (nothing sticky).

- **Provide some comfortable seating and allow some movement.** Students can bring in a soft pillow to sit on, or pillows can be placed on the floor. Rules need to be well established and practiced before the actual testing time so that no disturbance is caused. Those who need mobility can sit in the back of the room and allowed to quietly stand and stretch at designated intervals.

SOURCE: © National Reading Styles Institute, 1997.

preferences and strengths, they learn more easily and perform better on tests. We want our students to feel confident, relaxed, and energized as they prepare for and take tests. But if their reading styles are severely mismatched, they often feel tense, afraid, and even physically ill. Stress, frustration, and anxiety sap a child's ability to learn to read or test well—exactly what we don't want.

Unfortunately, tests are not fair. Some measure a host of minuscule reading skills that strongly global students do not need to become good readers. And many standardized reading achievement tests administered in the primary grades penalize students who are not strongly auditory and analytic. The phonics sections of reading tests often require the use of strong auditory skills. Students who cannot make the subtle distinctions among various letter sounds, associate those sounds with letters, and blend letter sounds quickly to form words are at a distinct disadvantage. While a knowledge of phonics is beneficial, students who have great difficulty learning phonics should not be penalized on reading achievement tests (Carbo, 1984, 1987, 1988).

To offset the disadvantage faced by many at-risk readers, it's important to use strategies that increase reading achievement sharply, help to compensate for student weaknesses, and reduce stress. The following strategies can be used to prepare students to take tests, as well as during the actual testing period. The first three strategies are important for raising students' reading skills; the last three increase energy and help to relax students.

BE STRATEGIC WHEN YOU PREPARE STUDENTS FOR TESTS

If you use your time strategically, you can prepare your students to do well on reading tests *without* taking an inordinate amount of teaching time. Test preparation should be enjoyable and educationally sound. When done well, the process of preparing students to take tests can improve voluntary reading and reading achievement. Some strategies should be used at the beginning of the school year; others can begin one or two months before the actual testing, and some are best used just a week or so prior to a test. Let's look now at strategic ways to prepare students for tests (Prell, 1986).

STRATEGIES TO USE AT THE BEGINNING OF THE SCHOOL YEAR

1. *Identify reading objectives.* Find out which objectives are being tested. Test booklets may list this information; as a last resort, your state education department or the testing companies that publish the tests usually will provide it. After learning which reading objectives are being tested, find out which of the test items are being emphasized. Some objectives may receive four test items, others 10 items, and so on. By looking at one student's test results, you can usually determine how many test items are used to measure a test objective. Test results are generally reported in fractions. If a student scores 6/10 in inferences, for example, then there are 10 inference items on the test and that youngster answered six correctly. Place your emphasis on teaching those objectives that represent the bulk of the test items.

2. *Determine which objectives to teach.* A good strategy here is to analyze prior test results to determine students' weakest areas. Look at the test objectives on which your students scored lowest. Were these objectives taught? Should they be retaught using materials that match the students' reading styles? If the answer is yes to either question, then these are objectives that should be taught through the students' strengths, which in most cases will be tactile and kinesthetic.

By the way, throughout the year make occasional use of test language such as "prior," "between," and "after" instead of first, second, third.

3. *Teach with hands-on materials.* Hands-on materials are a child-friendly way to teach test objectives. Tactile learners derive great benefit from practicing a specific skill with a tactile resource (Figures 12.2–12.4). After students master a skill with these resources, they can work on the skill in the more difficult format of a worksheet or test booklet. For at-risk readers, a good deal of time should be spent using tactile resources and much smaller amounts of time with worksheets. It's important to replicate the general format of the test when designing hands-on materials.

   Simple response cards can also be an effective way to involve students tactilely and kinesthetically. Suppose, for example, that students need to respond to test items with either a yes or no. Students could write a "Y" on one card with a marker, and an "N" on another. When the teacher or a student answers a question about a story or passage, each student could hold up a "Y" or an "N" depending on whether they agree or disagree with the answer. A more complex version of this strategy is to divide the class into teams. Each team receives cards with numbered reading questions. The team then decides on the answer to the first question, with one team member responsible for holding up the answer. (The teams all show their answer to the first question at the same time.) The teams with the correct answer score a point. Next, the second question is discussed by each team, and the game continues.

4. *Teach Test-Taking Strategies.* Many at-risk readers need to learn *how* to take tests. Here is a good strategy for developing comprehension skills. Assign students to work in pairs to read a sample comprehension item. First, the students read the passage together. Then they use the Highlighting Strategy, as follows:

   - *Highlight the question and the answer with the same color highlighting marker.* Using highlighting pens or markers, students highlight the first question. When they find the answer in the passage, they highlight the answer in the same color. Together they read the possible answers to the question, decide on the answer, and highlight it.

     The second question would be highlighted with a different color, and the same procedure followed. If the answer to the question is not directly stated, the students do not highlight the answer. In this way, students can see that inferential questions do not have definite answers within the passage. Add one, two, and then three passages to be completed before testing time, so that students become accustomed to working for longer periods of time.

- *Remove highlighters before test time.* Four to six weeks before testing, remove the highlighters if your state does not allow their use during the actual test, and request that students complete the activity in pairs without the highlighters. Finally, about two weeks before the test, have student complete this work alone.

  The highlighting strategy is especially helpful for tactile students. It also allows at-risk readers to work together, to search for information in context, to use color (which appeals especially to globals), and to discuss the answers. The student's time is spent learning the objective instead of randomly marking answers to the questions. It's an excellent reinforcement, too, because the answers seem to pop off the page.

STRATEGIES TO USE ABOUT TWO MONTHS BEFORE TESTING

1. *Use Carbo recordings.* With permission from copyright holders, record passages from past tests for students to practice. Students should listen and follow along in the story a few times. Then they can choral-read the passage back in groups, or read portions of the passage to a volunteer, teacher, or peer. This strategy can be done two to three times per week for about 15 minutes or so each day. Begin with easy stories and move up to more difficult ones. This practice will help to familiarize students with the types of stories on the test, the language of the stories, the story lengths, and the levels of difficulty that they can expect.

2. *Allow students to work in pairs to answer questions.* To reduce stress, have students work in pairs to practice answering the questions that follow the stories. These discussions often increase understanding. Discuss their answers and help them along the way with those items that they find difficult or confusing.

3. *Provide three different kinds of reading material.* There are essentially three types of reading passages on reading achievement tests: recreational reading (stories for fun), textual passages (science and social studies passages containing vocabulary specific to those subjects), and functional reading (which often requires students to interpret charts and graphs and follow directions). Students need to practice all three types of reading as well as the questions that follow. It is *not recommended* to provide this kind of practice throughout the school year, unless students want to read these materials. Remember that students (especially at-risk readers) have made unusually high reading gains when they can read books and stories that they *want to read.*

4. *Use hands-on materials to practice test questions.* These materials reduce stress, match the learning strengths of at-risk readers, and allow for

discussion of test items. Some suggestions are pictured in Figures 12.2–12.4. The electroboard in Figure 12.2 practices a functional reading skill, and the task cards in Figures 12.3 and 12.4 practice typical recreational reading skills.

Figure 12.2 Many functional questions involve interpreting graphs and charts. This electroboard provides tactile practice that is fun. Electroboards of this type can be created easily with Hot Dots®, which only require pressing down special dots on the card. See Appendix F for a source for Hot Dots.

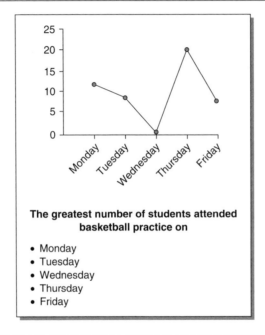

The greatest number of students attended basketball practice on

- Monday
- Tuesday
- Wednesday
- Thursday
- Friday

Figure 12.3 Task cards can be used to provide practice in a variety of reading skills, including antonyms. Simple 5" × 8" cards can be used to make the task cards.

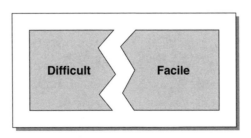

Figure 12.4   Multiple meanings of words (part of the vocabulary section of a test) can be practiced with Pic-Wizard™ cards, such as the one pictured. The student pokes through the hole next to the answer with a pencil, and self-checks on the back of the card. See Appendix F for the source for these cards.

Which word fits both sentences?

The signature on the check was_____.
He became an_____after the accident.

O wrong
O victim
O invalid
O paralytic

SOURCE: © 2001 Linda Queiruga, www.pic-wizard.com.

STRATEGIES TO USE TWO TO SIX WEEKS BEFORE TESTING

Generally, it's unwise to practice test items and test-taking strategies too far ahead of the actual test, because students become weary and turned off when this practice is overdone. Remember: Novelty engages the mind. By practicing only during the weeks right before a test, students are more likely to be interested in and remember what they practice (Prell, 1986).

1. *Introduce and use the language of the test* (about four to six weeks before the test). Skim through previous tests, reviewing with students any words they may not understand. Read directions to the students and discuss what the directions mean. Do this activity for about 10–15 minutes each day, if needed.

2. *Practice sample test items* (about four weeks before the test). As the test approaches, provide students with worksheets that closely resemble the actual test. This type of practice does help students to become familiar with a particular test format, but it has little effect on students' performance on other types of tests that are dissimilar to the one being practiced. This strategy should be used for very brief periods during the school day a few weeks before the test.

3. *Make students aware of the time allotted* (about two weeks before the test). Many students do not know how to use their time well. As the test nears, have students practice several test items within the confines of a specific amount of time. Place the time allotted on the board, and keep changing the amount of time remaining.

Figure 12.5   Using Bloom's Taxonomy to Improve Test Scores

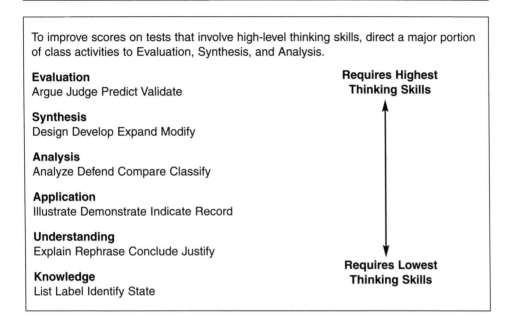

STRATEGIES TO USE ON TESTING DAYS

On testing days, if permitted, try to establish the environment and procedures that accommodate the reading styles of students, particularly at-risk
readers. Administer the test during the time of day when student energy is
highest. Allow students to bring in healthful snacks to eat and pillows to
put on their chairs. Provide a few pillows and rugs on the floor for those
who work best in an informal setting, and seat students with high mobility
needs in the back of the room so that they can stand and stretch as needed.

If you use these strategies, it's important to establish clear guidelines
and rehearse routines. Students are likely to feel better, test better, and
appreciate the thoughtful accommodations you have made.

A QUICK REVIEW: RECOMMENDATIONS
FOR TEACHERS

After receiving information about the test objectives, plan how you will teach
those objectives that are emphasized on the test. Phonics items are the exception. For some students, it may be a waste of time to try to teach and reteach
the phonics items. If the student is weak auditorially and only minimally
analytic, then that student may never be able to "hear" phonics. To some
degree, phonics is tested visually on an achievement test. Try working with

these students to notice visual patterns that might indicate the correct answer. A limited amount of time should be spent on this activity.

- Study the test results for your class from last year. Identify the at-risk readers with the lowest scores. Begin by teaching key test objectives through their perceptual strengths. Then increase the number of students for whom you are making this accommodation.
- Ask other teachers for strategies they use to teach objectives that your students have not mastered thoroughly.
- Try recording sample test passages. As your students work with these recordings, they will become familiar with the test language and the levels of the material to be read.
- Remember that low-performing students are often tactile/kinesthetic youngsters. Teach test objectives through recordings, games, and kinesthetic activities. After the objectives have been mastered by the students within a game format, transfer the material to the paper-and-pencil format. As testing dates grow nearer (within a few weeks), provide practice with worksheets that closely resemble the test.

We all know that test scores count. But our children and their future count much more. Place test practice in its place—give it only small amounts of your precious teaching time. Keep focused on the real reason that you became a teacher: to help your students learn to read and comprehend at high levels and enjoy reading so that they read a great deal voluntarily. As your students read more and more, the chance that they will do well on reading tests increases. Use the strategies in this book and in this chapter to accomplish these most important goals *and* to achieve high test scores.

Epilogue

Becoming a Great Teacher of Reading

You have the power within you to become a great teacher of reading. It's all there, waiting to be released. What's important is to begin the journey. It doesn't matter whether you take small steps or big steps. Just begin moving in the right direction, and as you do you will gain momentum and strength. Your successes will propel you forward; they will transform you and your students. Believe that your students can succeed; feel it in your heart, and let that belief guide and sustain your efforts.

When I began working with students who had learning disabilities, I thought I could teach reading very well. I was wrong. It wasn't until I really watched, listened, and understood my students that I realized I had so much to learn and try if I was going to truly help them. I knew they had the intelligence to learn to read; in the deepest part of me, I believed in them. That deep belief changed my teaching. It helped me to realize that whatever teaching had taken place before I met my students had not tapped into their intelligence. Most of their teachers had used more and more of the same strategies that didn't work—and then, finally, given up.

Don't ever give up. And when today's insanity surrounds you—the continual testing, the mandates, the endless worksheets, the hundreds of skills, the mounds of paperwork, and all the agendas that have nothing to do with helping our students learn to read—don't allow this insanity to separate you from your students. Be aware of the barriers that can prevent you from doing what's right for children. Keep believing that your students can succeed. See them as they truly are. They all want to learn to read, and they need you to help them.

Above all, believe in yourself and stay strong. You are their teacher. You work with the children, and you can make the greatest difference in their lives and their future. Research tells us this, but you already knew it. This is why you became a teacher in the first place.

The strategies in this book will help you teach your students to read, to love reading, and to do well on achievement tests. Try these strategies, use them, improve them—anything that helps your students learn to read with ease and enjoyment.

But remember, it is the way you touch your students' lives every day that matters most—their hearts, their minds, their belief in themselves. Trust your heart, your intuition, the force of your will, and your talents. Put your students first, honor their strengths, respect their interests, and believe in their ability to learn.

Believe that all students can learn to read, because they *can*. They learn when we tap into their strongest learning pathways, use reading materials that truly interest them, and use whatever reading methods help them learn to read with ease and enjoyment. I wish you the joy of exploration, discovery, and success. Once you begin this journey of becoming a great teacher of reading, it becomes a passion. Make it *your* passion. *You* make the difference. Make the grand difference.

Appendix A

Glossary

Active Learning—Learning experiences in which the students are active physically, such as touching, acting, and walking (see Chapter 8).

Analytic Learners—Tend to be highly rational, logical, detail-oriented; enjoy highly organized teaching (see Chapter 4).

Assisted Reading Methods—A group of reading methods in which a more experienced reader reads and is then imitated by the novice reader (see Chapter 6).

Attention-Deficit/Hyperactivity Disorder (ADHD)—Students who use motion to bring their central nervous system to a normal state of arousal or alertness (see Chapter 11).

Auditory Activity—An activity that requires of the learner any or all of the following auditory abilities: memory, discrimination, sequential memory (see Chapter 4).

Auditory Learners—Learn by listening and speaking; recall what they hear; usually enjoy discussions (see Chapter 4).

Carbo Recording Method—A method of recording small portions of a high-interest, challenging story at a slow pace in order to increase reading enjoyment, fluency, vocabulary, and comprehension (see Chapter 7).

Choral Reading—Two or more individuals read a passage in unison. Often verse or patterned language is read by alternating lines or passages (see Chapter 6).

Colored Overlays—Thin sheets of specially treated plastic of specific colors that have been found to help many individuals with visual problems (see Chapter 10).

Critical Thinking—Judging the accuracy, validity, and quality of ideas; using sound criteria, logical analysis, and judgment (see Chapter 12).

Deficit Model—A theory of instruction that attempts to teach students to read through their weakest modality. One common practice in this model is to teach students who are weak auditorially with intensive, systematic phonics instruction (see Chapters 5 and 10).

Differentiated Instruction—A teaching approach that uses diverse instructional strategies to benefit all learners, including those who are racially, culturally, and linguistically diverse, and those with a range of skills, gifts, strengths, needs, abilities, and disabilities.

Dyslexia—There are two distinct types of dyslexia: visual dyslexia and auditory dyslexia. Students with visual dyslexia often see letters and numbers that reverse, swirl, or slide off the page. Students with auditory dyslexia often have problems processing language or associating letters with their sounds, blending sounds, and recalling what they hear (see Chapter 10).

Echo Reading—The teacher reads a sentence or passage with good expression; then the student reads the same material back, imitating the teacher (see Chapter 6).

Emotional Disturbances—Emotional, behavioral, or mental disorders that make learning difficult for the youngster and/or have an adverse impact on his/her relationships with peers and teachers (see Chapter 11).

English Language Learners (ELL)—Students whose native language is not English and who have not yet achieved mastery of the English language (see Chapter 11).

Fernald Reading Method—A word that a youngster wants to learn is written on a large card by the teacher with a crayon. The youngster traces over and says the word two or three times, and then writes the word from memory (see Chapter 5).

Five Reading Areas—The National Reading Panel (NRP) has identified these five reading areas: phonemics, phonics, fluency, vocabulary, and comprehension. The first four reading areas all serve one purpose: to increase comprehension (see Chapter 3).

Global Learners—Tend to be strongly emotional, intuitive, group-oriented; highly responsive to holistic teaching (see Chapter 4).

Individualized Reading Method—Students choose what they want to read. As each student reads alone, the teacher holds individual conferences at which the child reads aloud and discusses what he or she has read. The teacher keeps detailed records of the child's interests and skill levels. Small groups of students with similar reading interests or skill needs may be formed from time to time (see Chapter 5).

Kinesthetic Activity—An activity involving physical movement such as jumping or walking; an activity that promotes learning through large-muscle movement (see Chapter 4).

Kinesthetic Learners—Learn through whole-body movement; recall what they experience; often enjoy building, acting, direct experience (see Chapter 4).

Language-Experience Method—Initially, individuals or groups of students dictate stories about their experiences to their teacher. Later, students learn to read what they write themselves about their experiences (see Chapter 5).

Learning Disability—A disorder in the processes by which the brain understands or uses language, occurring in students with average or above average intelligence.

Learning Styles—Ways in which people learn. Commonly known elements include visual, auditory, tactile, and kinesthetic (see Chapter 4 and Appendix D).

Linguistic Method—Word families or patterns (fat, cat, mat) are taught and used in beginning stories (see Chapter 5).

Mobility—A need some students have to move often as they learn (see Chapters 8 and 9).

National Assessment of Educational Progress (NAEP). A national test mandated by Congress, which is administered to a large sampling of students in the United States yearly to assess their progress in reading and mathematics (see Chapter 1 and Appendix B).

Neurological Impress Method—The teacher sits behind the youngster and reads into the child's ear as the child attempts to read in unison. The child holds the book. The teacher sets the pace by tracing with his or her finger below the words (see Chapter 6).

No Child Left Behind Act (NCLB)—Signed into law in 2002, its objective is to close the achievement gap in grades K–3 at the time of this writing, especially for poor, ESL, and underachieving students (see Appendix B).

Orton-Gillingham Method—A multisensory form of phonics that is highly structured and emphasizes tactile input (see Chapter 5).

Paired Reading—Two people take turns reading the same passage. A variety of pairs can be used, including two students and a teacher and a student (see Chapter 6).

Phonics—Students learn isolated letter sounds and then blend them to form words (see Chapters 3 and 5).

Reading First—The reading initiative that provides guidelines and funding for the implementation of the No Child Left Behind Act (see Appendix B).

Reading Styles—The application of learning style theory to the teaching of reading, with implications for reading instruction (see Chapters 4 and 5, and Appendix C).

Shared Reading—The teacher reads a story or passage while pointing to the words. Often an enlarged book, a chart, or a passage on a chalkboard or overhead transparency is used (see Chapter 6).

Tactile Activity—An activity involving touch, such as tracing sandpaper letters, playing a board game, folding paper; an activity that promotes learning through touching and feeling with the hands (see Chapter 8).

Tactile Learners—Learn by touching; recall what they touch; enjoy games and manipulating objects (see Chapter 4).

Visual Activity—An activity that stimulates the visual sense through color, shape, and other visual stimuli; an activity that promotes learning through sight (see Chapter 4).

Visual Learners—Learn by observing; recall what they see; notice details; enjoy demonstrations (see Chapter 4).

Whole-Word Method—Before students read a story, key words that may be unfamiliar are introduced, often on flash cards, word lists, and in the context of sentences (see Chapter 5).

Appendix B

U.S. Reading Achievement

WHERE WE ARE

According to the latest data available from the National Assessment of Educational Progress (NAEP), the percentage of our students who read at the proficient level (at or above grade level) has not improved and is appallingly low. Less than one-third of U.S. students in grades 4, 8, and 12, and only 31% of U.S. college graduates tested at the proficient level.

In addition, reading for pleasure continues to decline each year (Dillon, 2005a). Boys fall 1½ years behind girls in reading between grades 8 and 12, and males make up an increasingly smaller percentage of U.S. college students (Newkirk, 2003). Finally, though a high percentage of U.S. students perform at the proficient reading level on their state exams, a very low percentage perform at that level on the more valid and accurate NAEP (Ravitch, 2005).

Two Sobering Events

Our extremely low literacy rates have an exceedingly negative impact on the U.S. educational system and the economy. Consider these two sobering events:

1. In 2005, Toyota closed its plant in Alabama and replaced it by opening a plant in Ontario, Canada, despite the sizable financial incentives available in the United States. Toyota cited the high quality of the Ontario work force compared to the disappointing quality and low literacy of the Alabama work force. Jobs were lost, tax revenue was lost, and future jobs were put in jeopardy (Krugman, 2005).

Figure B.1   Ominous Trends in Reading

- Less than one-third of Grade 4, 8, and 12 students read at or above grade level according to the regular NAEP assessment of 2005 (Bracey, 2006).

- Between Grades 4 and 8, boys fall behind girls in reading by 1½ years. Since 1980, boys' dislike for school has risen 71% (Newkirk, 2003).

- Only 44% of college students are men—they're now a minority. A major cause is the low literacy rates of boys (Tyre, 2006).

- Only 31% of college graduates demonstrate reading proficiency (Dillon, 2005b).

- International competition is growing lightning fast compared to the academic growth of U.S. students (Friedman, 2005).

Figure B.2   Percentage of Students Reading at the Proficient Level on the National Assessment of Educational Progress (NAEP), 1992–2005

	4th Grade	8th Grade
1992	29%	29%
1994	30%	30%
1998	31%	33%
1998	29%	32%
2000	29%	
2002	31%	33%
2003	31%	32%
2005	31%	31%

SOURCE: Adapted from Greg Toppo, "Math Proficiency Rises, but Reading Stagnates," *USA Today,* October 20, 2005, p. 7D.

2. International competition is growing lightning fast compared to the stagnating reading scores of U.S. students. As a group, American students graduating from high school or college and entering the work force are increasingly *less* literate. Robert L. Wehling, a retired global-marketing officer, warns us of the "devastating consequences" for our country caused by our low literacy rates, stating:

> I've been watching very, very closely the educational progress in Asia—China, India, Vietnam, Singapore, and several others . . . they're making rapid progress, whereas we're making miniscule progress. And I don't think the average American understands the impact of this for our future, because they're going to have the bulk of the intellectual and creative talent in the world, and that has devastating consequences for us. (Olson, 2005, p. 24)

THE IMPACT OF READING FIRST

In January 2002, President Bush signed into law the No Child Left Behind Act (NCLB). The overriding objective of NCLB is to close the achievement gap in Grades K–3, especially for children who are poor, ESL, and/or underachievers. NCLB defines "good" schools as those that are effective with every group of children they serve. Few would argue the merits of NCLB's important goal. However, educators' major concerns include a lack of funds to implement the law, impossibly high standards, an over-emphasis on reading and math to the detriment of other subjects, and an overly narrow definition of success (passing annual tests) (Franklin, 2006). Objections from educators have been so strong that the task force of the National Conference of State Legislatures said in its panel's report that the "federal government's role has become excessively intrusive in the day-to-day operations of public education." They added that the "task force does not believe that N. C. L. B. is constitutional" (Dillon, 2005c, p. 1).

Reading First Investigated

More objections are likely to come forth based on a continuing government audit of the U.S. Department of Education. The department's Inspector General found that "Department of Education officials violated conflict of interest rules when awarding grants to states under President Bush's billion-dollar reading initiative [Reading First], and steered contracts to favored textbook publishers" (Dillon, 2006, p. 1). The report also said that members of review panels were improperly selected and awarded large grants, often failing to detect conflicts of interest. In one e-mail message cited in the report, the director of Reading First, Chris Doherty, told his staff members to make it clear to a particular company that it was not favored by the department. Doherty wrote: "They are trying to crash our party and we need to beat the [expletive deleted] out of them in front of all the other would-be party crashers who are standing on the front lawn waiting to see how we welcome these dirtbags" (Dillon, 2006, p. 1). Mr. Doherty has since resigned from the U.S. Department of Education.

Responding to this audit, the International Reading Association issued a press release stating that "the IG's report directly quotes individual communications to establish that there was a plan to direct the outcomes of independent panels, stack those panels with those who already had formed a bias, and promote specific reading programs, while eliminating others" cite truncated. ("IRA Responds," 2006, p. 1). Note: Reading First funds are meant to be used for reading programs with a strong "scientific," published, research base that demonstrates that use of the program has produced substantial reading gains.

NAEP Scores Are Static or Have Declined

Most important, has reading achievement improved during the period of time that NCLB has been implemented, especially for the youngest students tested by the NAEP, our nine-year-olds? NCLB was passed by Congress in 2001 and signed into law in 2002. Therefore, analysis of the data would have to begin with the year 2002. When that is done, scores on the NAEP remained static or went down during the period of NCLB's implementation, according to Gerald Bracey (2006). Bracey analyzed the regular NAEP 2005 assessments and found that "fourth-grade reading reached the same level as it had at the onset of NCLB in 2002 . . . the proportion of students at or above the proficient level was static for fourth-graders at 31% and fell for eighth-graders from 33% to 31%" (p. 152). (Note: The NAEP 2005 has the most current NAEP data available at the time of this writing.) On a positive note, Bracey did report a slight gain in the reading scores of nine-year-old African American and Hispanic students.

In summary, NCLB's focus on closing the achievement gap is important. However, since the law was enacted, overall, the reading achievement of U.S. students has remained static or declined. Currently, less than one-third of our students read at or above grade level. Critics of NCLB say it has funding problems and a narrow definition of success and overemphasizes end-of-year testing. In addition, a recent audit of the Department of Education revealed that Reading First funds were distributed illegally to a narrow group of favored publishers.

Appendix C

Reading Styles Research

The strategies in this book are used extensively in the Carbo Reading Styles Program (CRSP). Many of the research studies described in this section are available with graphed results at www.nrsi.com. Available at that same Web site are listings of model schools and model classrooms that have implemented the CRSP strategies at a high level.

NATIONAL AND REGIONAL RECOGNITION

During the past decade, the Carbo Reading Styles Program (CRSP) has been recognized for its positive effect on improving students' reading achievement in Grades K–12 (see Figure C.1). After extensive evaluations, the Northwest Regional Lab (funded by the U.S. Dept. of Education) listed CRSP in its *Catalog of School Reform Models* in 1998, in 2002, and in 2006. To be considered for listing in this catalog, invited programs are required to submit 10 research studies conducted on their program. The criteria for inclusion in the *Catalog of School Reform Models* are:

- evidence of effectiveness in improving student academic achievement;
- widespread replication with organizational capacity to continue gearing up;
- high-quality implementation assistance to schools; and comprehensiveness.

In 1997 the Kentucky Department of Education included CRSP in its Results-Based Showcase, which featured reading programs that had demonstrated high reading gains. (Results-Based Showcase, 1997–1998), and in 1999 CRSP was listed as one of six reading programs selected for the Milken Foundation's book *Reading Programs That Work: Programs for Pre-Kindergarten to 4th Grade* (Schacter, 1999). The Milken book included reading programs that "helped students learn to read better than traditional methods" and are "driven by reading research, not ideology" (p. 7). In that same year, CRSP was selected for inclusion in *A Guide to Research-Based Programs and Practices for Improving Literacy,* prepared by the New England Comprehensive Center (NECAC). One year later, in 2000, CRSP was selected by the Education Commission of the States for *ECS's List of Promising Practices in Reading.*

In 2002, CRSP was selected and listed in *What Works in the Elementary Grades: Results-Based Staff Development,* published by the National Staff Development Council (Killion, 2002b). Killion stated CRSP "has demonstrated its impact on student achievement . . . offers intensive up-front professional development and an array of follow up support . . . [and is] adaptable to nearly any school context and appropriate for any type of learner . . . grade 1 to middle levels" (p. 49).

Figure C.1   National and Regional Recognition of the Carbo Reading Styles Program (CRSP)

Based on published research studies on CRSP, the program has been selected for the high quality of its research base, teaching practices, and staff development by

Northwest Regional Lab (1998, 2002, 2006) (funded by the U.S. Dept. of Education). CRSP was selected and listed as one of three research-based language arts programs in its *Catalog of School Reform Models.*

Education Commission of the States (2000). CRSP was included in ECS's *List of Promising Practices in Reading.*

National Staff Development Council (2002). CRSP was included in its publication *What Works in the Elementary Grades* (Killion, 2002b).

Milken Foundation (2000). CRSP was one of six reading programs included in its publication *Reading Programs That Work: A Review of Programs for Pre-Kindergarten to 4th Grade* (Schacter, 2000).

New England Comprehensive Center (1999). CRSP was included in the Center's manual: *A Guide to Research-Based Programs and Practices for Improving Early Literacy.*

Phi Delta Kappa Study (1998). Students of CRSP-trained teachers achieved higher scores on standardized achievement tests six times more frequently than their controls (Carbo, Barber, & Thomasson, 1998).

RESEARCH SUMMARY

More than 15 years of research indicates that when schools accommodate students' reading styles, students improve significantly in reading motivation and achievement, school attendance increases, and discipline problems and retentions decrease significantly. These results have been reported by educators involved in classroom and schoolwide implementation of CRSP in Grades K–12 (Acceleration Program, 1998; Bradsby, Wise, Mundell, & Haas, 1992; Brooks, 1991; Barber, Carbo, & Thomasson, 1998; Hodgin & Wooliscroft, 1997; LaShell, 1986; Langford, 2000; Molbeck, 1994; Oglesby & Suter, 1995; O'Tuel & Holt, 1992; Skipper, 1997; Snyder, 1993, 1997).

In 1998 Phi Delta Kappa published a two-year study of CRSP involving 561 students in Grades 1 to 6 from six school districts in six states (Barber, Carbo, & Thomasson, 1998). The study compared the effectiveness of many different reading programs to CRSP and found that, when implemented at the 85% level or higher, CRSP was significantly more effective than extant programs. In this carefully controlled quasi-experimental study, both experimental and control teachers and students were matched. Districts used their own standardized achievement tests to measure reading results. The findings indicated that, after two years of implementation, students of the CRSP-trained teachers achieved higher effect sizes on the reading subtests measured six times more frequently than did the students of the control teachers.

Note: Leading the research team for this study was Larry Barber, then director of research for Phi Delta Kappa. All data from this research study were sent directly from the schools involved to Dr. Barber, who analyzed the data and reported the results of the study. Every district involved had two people who had been trained in research design and data collection by Dr. Barber, and who worked closely with him. Copies of this study are available at www.nrsi.com.

The doctoral research of Suter was described in an article by Oglesby and Suter (1995). Suter's study involved 198 third and sixth graders. All subjects were pre- and posttested with the Gates-MacGinitie Reading Test. After six months, the CRSP group made significantly higher reading gains than their controls.

Ninety students with learning disabilities in Grades 1–6 participated in LaShell's (1986) study—42 from the Lake Stevens School District and 48 from the Arlington School District, both in Washington state. Within eight months, the CRSP students gained 15 months in reading comprehension; the control students gained four months. That difference was significant at the .001 level. The reading styles students also achieved a significantly higher internal locus of control (at the .001 level) than the control group, indicating that the CRSP students felt significantly more responsible for their actions, while the control students believed more strongly that results are caused by powerful outside forces.

Brooks (1991) reported higher gains in oral reading comprehension and significantly higher gains in silent reading comprehension for CRSP students ($p < .01$), compared to their controls. The subjects for this one-semester study were 42 Chapter 1 students in grades 2 to 6 who scored at or below the 36th percentile in reading on the Metropolitan Achievement Tests.

In 1986 the Bledsoe County Schools in Tennessee averaged a stanine score of only three in reading—not unusual for a rural school district in a poverty area. After implementing CRSP for three years, the system equaled state and national averages in reading (approximately the fifth stanine) (Snyder, 1993). In 1992 the school district was honored with the Governor's Award for Excellence in Education. The Bledsoe County district is a 1,700-student system in the mountains of eastern Tennessee. The county's per-capita income was $8,000 in 1994, with approximately 50% to 70% of the students considered to be at risk of failure.

Snyder (1997) conducted a second study with 282 students drawn from grades 3, 4, 6, 7, and 8. The CRSP subjects in all grades under study significantly outperformed students in the control group in total reading as measured by the California Tests of Basic Skills (CTB4), after both the first and second years of the study. Snyder also found that, compared to the controls, the experimental Chapter 1 group had significantly higher social studies scores.

Significantly higher reading gains were also reported by O'Tuel and Holt (1992) for the students of CRSP-trained teachers compared to their controls. The control district was selected by the South Carolina Department of Education. This experiment took place over one school year and involved all fifth and sixth graders in two participating school districts.

The results reported by Hodgin and Wooliscroft (1997) took place over a period of one year and involved 22 third-grade inclusion students. After implementing CRSP for one year, the authors found that the percentage of students passing the test objectives on the Texas Assessment of Academic Skills (TAAS) rose from 41% to 86%.

In 1997 Skipper reported that only 21% of elementary students in the Uvalde School District were passing the TAAS. After three years of CRSP, that figure rose to nearly 70% passing the TAAS. Two experiments were conducted in Uvalde to test the effectiveness of the program. The first occurred during the summer of 1994 with 42 first graders considered to be highly at risk of being retained. After the six-week CRSP program, the first-grade retention rate dropped from 8.9% to 1.7%. In six weeks, the youngsters gained more than 3.5 months in reading. The second experiment took place at Robb Elementary School in 1994–95. At the end of the school year, the percentage of students passing the state reading test rose from 46% to 73%. Seventy-eight percent of the students in the Uvalde district were Hispanic, many had limited proficiency in English, and 75% came from families considered economically disadvantaged.

Similarly positive results were reported by Langford (2000) in a report to the National Reading Styles Institute for Paterson Elementary School, an inner-city K–6 school in Montgomery, Alabama. Most residents in the Paterson School District were unemployed. The enrollment was 99.7% African-American, 99.9% of the families live at or below the poverty level as defined by the U.S. government, and 100% of the students received free or reduced-cost lunch. After two years of CRSP (from 1998 to 2000), students in grades 1–6 gained an average of 9.5 percentiles in their total reading scores on the SAT-9. In the spring of 1999, Paterson met its academic objective, moving from an Alert II status to a Caution status (*Carbo Reading Styles Program: Research Update*, 2000).

More recently, two CRSP model schools, Marion Elementary School (Marion, MI) and Ocean City Elementary School (Ft. Walton Beach, FL), reported the following results. In 2001, 42.1% of fourth graders at Marion Elementary scored at the proficient reading level on their state test (MEAP). After three years of implementing CRSP, the percentage of fourth graders scoring at the proficient level in reading rose to 87% in 2005, and to 95% in 2006. Marion Elementary is a rural school with a 99% White student population, 61% of whom qualify for free or reduced-cost lunch. There is high unemployment in the area (one-third of families have no phones).

Ocean City Elementary's scores on the Florida state test advanced significantly after three years of CRSP, exceeding both the district and state averages. The student population at Ocean City Elementary is 70% low socioeconomic and 30% ESE. By 2005 the school closed the reading gap between their White students (from 65% proficient in 2003 to 73% proficient in 2005) and African American students (from 50% proficient in 2003 to 72% in 2005). And they narrowed the reading gap for the students with economic disadvantages and learning disabilities.

Reading gains with CRSP have not been limited to elementary youngsters. Thornton Township District 205, in Thornton, Illinois, used CRSP to improve the reading skills of 226 remedial students in its high school English Acceleration Program. These were students who lacked the basic skills to function in their academic high school classes. After nine months of CRSP, the students averaged an 11.6 NCE growth in reading as measured by the Gates-MacGinitie Reading Test, and 56% of the students were able to move into regular English classes (Acceleration Program, 1998).

Appendix D

Learning Styles Research

This appendix contains highlights from the research on the Dunn and Dunn Model of Learning Styles. Since my work in reading styles is based on that model, it is appropriate to describe some of the important research on the Dunn and Dunn Model.

DESCRIPTION OF THE DUNN AND DUNN MODEL

The Dunn and Dunn Model of Learning Styles describes a person's learning strengths and preferences while learning, and considers how a student's ability to learn is affected by the: (1) immediate environment, and the learner's (2) emotional makeup, (3) sociological preferences, (4) physical needs, and (5) style of processing information.

Although there are several learning-style models, only three address more than one of two variables on a bipolar continuum. Of those three, only the Dunn and Dunn Model, developed at St. John's University, has been university-based for three decades and has an extensive research base (DeBello, 1990; Tendy & Geisert, 1998–1999).

Thirty Years of Research

Practitioners throughout the United States have reported significantly improved student attitudes and higher achievement on standardized tests after implementing the Dunn and Dunn Model. These gains have been documented for low-achieving and special education students in urban, suburban, and rural schools (Brunner & Majewski, 1990; Cain & Norwood, 2000; Dunn & DeBello, 1999; Dunn & Dunn, 2005; Elliot, 1991).

A meta-analysis of 42 experimental studies conducted at 13 universities with the Dunn and Dunn Model between 1980 and 1990 revealed that eight variables coded for each study produced 65 individual effect sizes (Dunn, Griggs, Olson, Gorman, & Beasley, 1995). The overall, unweighted group effect size value (r) was .384; the weighted effect size value was .353 with a mean difference (d) of .755. Referring to the normal curve, these results suggest that students whose learning styles were accommodated achieved 75% of a standard deviation higher academic scores than students whose learning styles were not accommodated.

More than 500 research publications and at least 100 published practitioners' reports indicate that identifying and accommodating the learning styles of poorly achieving students with the Dunn and Dunn Model leads to statistically higher standardized achievement test scores than traditional teaching (Dunn & Dunn, 2005; *Research on the Dunn and Dunn Model*, 2000).

The Dunn and Dunn Model has a long-term record of improving student achievement and attitudes. For example, according to the U.S. Center for Research in Education (CRE), the 20-year period of extensive federal funding (1979–1990) produced very few programs that resulted in statistically higher standardized achievement test scores for special education students (Alberg et al., 1992). Prominent among the few programs that consistently increased achievement was the Dunn and Dunn Model.

FOR MORE INFORMATION . . .

To obtain more information on the Dunn and Dunn Model, go to www.learningstyles.net, which contains a bibliography of more than 850 citations of studies conducted by researchers at 125 different universities. The learning-style studies conducted at those institutions received "23 national and international awards for the quality of their research" (Dunn & Dunn, 1999, pp. 205–206). In addition, a recent book by Dunn and Griggs (2003, 2004) includes descriptions of every aspect of the Dunn and Dunn Model, with updated research, text, tables, and references.

Appendix E

Reading Style Inventory® (RSI)
Grade 1 to Adult

The *Reading Style Inventory* (RSI) (Carbo, 1982, 1994) is a questionnaire that describes a student's learning style for reading and recommends the most compatible reading strategies for that individual. The RSI takes about 30 minutes to administer on computer or in a printed version of the questionnaire.

For more information, go to www.nrsi.com.

RSI INDIVIDUAL PROFILES

RSI Individual Profiles describe a student's reading style strengths and weaknesses, and recommend the most compatible reading strategies, methods, and materials for that student. Additional information describing the reading strategies and methods can be printed.

The following two kinds of RSI Individual Profiles can be generated.

- One-Page Condensed Report (Figure E.2)
- Three-Page Complete Report (not shown)

An example of the condensed report is shown below.

RSI GROUP PROFILES

RSI Group Profiles describe a group's reading style strengths and weaknesses, and recommend the most effective reading strategies for that group and for the individual students within the group.

Figure E.1   Elements of Reading Style Identified by the Reading Style Inventory®

I.	**Environmental Stimuli**	**Does the student read best:**
	SOUND	with music, with talking, or in silence?
	LIGHT	in bright or dim light?
	TEMPERATURE	in a warm or cool temperature?
	DESIGN	in a formal design (hard chair at a desk) or an informal design (soft chair, rug, floor)?
II.	**Emotional Stimuli**	**When reading, is the student:**
	MOTIVATION	self-motivated, not self-motivated, motivated by peers, motivated by adults?
		Does the student:
	PERSISTENCE	complete reading tasks?
	RESPONSIBILITY	do the work agreed upon or assigned?
	STRUCTURE	prefer little or much direction, many or few choices of reading materials, require time limits?
III.	**Sociological Stimuli**	**Does the student read best**
	PEERS	with five or six students?
	SELF	alone?
	PAIR	with one other student?
	TEAM	with three students?
	ADULT	with a teacher, parent, administrator, etc.?
	VARIED	with combinations of students and adults?
IV.	**Physical Stimuli**	**Does the student read best:**
	PERCEPTUAL	when taught through his or her visual modality, auditory modality, tactile modality, kinesthetic modality, and/or with a multisensory approach?
	INTAKE	when permitted to eat and drink while learning?
	TIME	in the early morning, late morning, early afternoon, late afternoon, evening?
	MOBILITY	when permitted to move while learning?
V.	**Psychological Stimuli**	**Does the student:**
	GLOBAL/ANALYTIC	learn best when information is presented holistically (globally) and/or logically, step-by-step (analytically)?

Figure E.2   Condensed RSI Individual Profile. This one-page RSI profile describes a student's global and analytic tendencies and perceptual strengths, top three recommended reading methods and materials, and top five recommended teaching strategies.

Grade: 6
Teacher's Name: Mary Downing

Student Name: Paul Wendell
Date: 09-27-2004

Global/Analytic Tendencies
Very Strong global tendencies
Minimal analytic tendencies

Perceptual Strengths
Excellent auditory strengths
Fair visual strengths
Good tactile strengths
Excellent kinesth strengths

Recommended Reading Methods
Carbo Recorded-Book method
Individualized method
Phonics and linguistic methods

Recommended Reading Materials
Manipulative w/large-muscle movement, floor games
Trade books, magazines, short stories
Recorded readings above student's reading level

Recommended Teaching Strategies
Allow discussion, oral reports
Allow student demonstrations
Use high-interest stories
Try colored overlays
Limit true/false, multiple choice items

Special Modifications for This Student, the following modification are recommended for this student:
For all reading methods, give to student
Write directions for work, give to student
Use cursive to lesson b and d reversals
Provide repetition of words through many senses
Have students sound out words while reading
Limit board copying, give written copy of assignment
Try colored overlay page

The following four kinds of RSI Group Profiles can be generated:

- One-Page Condensed Profile (not shown)
- Two-Page Summary Profile (see Figure 9.4)
- 24-Page Names Profile (not shown)
- 16-Page X's Profile (not shown)

RELIABILITY OF THE READING STYLE INVENTORY®

A series of test-retest reliability studies were conducted with the RSI from 1981 through 1994, as the instrument evolved. In the 1994 studies, students were drawn from inner-city, suburban, and rural areas. The samples also represented good, average, and poor readers. A three-week test-retest was observed in each case. These are the results of the most recent studies.

Reading Style Inventory, Grades 1–2

In a sample of 183 first and second graders, reliability coefficients for the RSI-P subscales ranged from .73 to .91, with an average of .81. The highest-reliability coefficient average was obtained for the perceptual subscales.

Reading Style Inventory, Grades 3–8

In a sample of 216 students in Grades 3–8, reliability coefficients for the RSI-I subscales ranged from .69 to .88, with an average of .87. The highest-reliability coefficient average was obtained for the perceptual subscales.

Reading Style Inventory, Grades 9–Adult

In a sample of 122 students in Grades 9–adult, reliability coefficients for the RSI-P subscales ranged from .71 to .92, with an average of .86. The highest-reliability coefficient average was obtained for the perceptual subscales.

Appendix F

Sources for Educational Materials Discussed in This Book

Color Overlays
  Available at www.dyslexiacure.com

Flip Chute Template
  Available at www.learningstyles.net

Hot Dots
  Available at www.educationalinsights.com

Pic-Wizard Vocabulary Cards
  Available at www.pic-wizard.com

Power Reading Program
  Available at www.nrsi.com

Reading Games
  Available at www.nrsi.com

Sight Words That Stick® by Janet Martin
  Available at www.nrsi.com

Stories Recorded Using the Carbo Method
  Available at www.nrsi.com

Training and Awareness Videos for Assessing Visual Dyslexia
  Available at www.seeitright.com, www.dyslexiacure.com

References

Acceleration program. (1998, December). *Thornton Township District 205 newsletter,* Thornton, IL.

Adams, M. J. (1990) *Beginning to read: Thinking and learning about print.* Cambridge, MA: MIT Press.

Adler, L., & Atwood, M. (1987). *Poor readers: What do they really see on the page? A study of a major cause of dyslexia.* Los Angeles: Los Angeles County Office of Education.

A guide to research-based programs and practices for improving early literacy (1999, October). Newton, MA: New England Comprehensive Assistance Center and the Education Development Center, Inc.

Alberg, J., Cook, L., Fiore, T., Friend, M., & Sano, S. (1992). *Educational approaches and options for integrating students with disabilities: A decision tool.* Triangle Park, NC: Research Triangle Institute.

Allington, R. L. (2001). *What really matters for struggling readers: Designing research-based programs.* New York: Longman.

Allington, R. L. (1991). The legacy of "Slow it down and make it more concrete." In J. Zutell & S. McCormick (Eds.), *Learner factors/teacher factors: Issues in Literacy research and instruction (40th Yearbook of the National Reading Conference,* pp. 19–30). Chicago: National Reading Conference.

Allington, R. L. (1983). The reading instruction provided readers of differing abilities. *Elementary School Journal, 83,* 548–559.

Anderson, L. W., & Pellicer, L. O. (1990). Synthesis of research on compensatory and remedial education. *Educational Leadership, 48*(1), 10–16.

Anderson, R. C. (1996). Research foundations to support wide reading. In V. Greaney (Ed.), *Promoting reading in developing countries* (pp. 55–77). Newark, DE: International Reading Association.

Anderson, R. C., Hiebert, E. H., Scott, J. A., & Wilkinson, I. A. G. (1985). *Becoming a nation of readers.* Washington, D C.: The National Institute of Education.

Anglin, D. (1996, November 17). Reading program changes students lives. *Mississippi Press,* pp. 1C–2C.

Applebee, A. N., Langer, J. A., & Mullis, I. V. S. (1988). *Who reads best? Factors related to reading achievement in grades 3, 7, and 11* (Report No: 17-R-01). Princeton, NJ: Educational Testing Service.

Armstrong, T. (1998). *Awakening genius in the classroom.* Alexandria, VA: Association for Curriculum and Development.

Ashton-Warner, S. (1963). *Teacher.* New York: Simon & Schuster.

Atchinson, M. K., & Brown, D. M. (1988). *The relationship between the learning styles and reading achievement of sixth-grade students in the state of Alabama.* Paper presented at the annual meeting of the Mid-South Educational Research Association (ERIC Document Reproduction Service No. ED 300 722).

Aurback, E. (1995). Critical issues: Deconstructing the discourse of strengths in family literacy. *JRB: A Journal of Literacy, 27,* 643–661.

Barber, L., Carbo, M., & Thomasson, R. (1998). *A comparative study of the reading styles program to extant programs of teaching reading.* Bloomington, IN: Phi Delta Kappa.

Barkley, R. (1990). *Attention deficit hyperactivity disorder.* New York: Guilford Press.

Beck, I., & McKeown, M. (1991). Conditions of vocabulary acquisition. In R. Barr, M. L. Kamil, P. Mosenthal, & P. D. Pearson (Eds.), *Handbook of reading research: Vol. II* (pp. 789–814). Mahwah, NJ: Lawrence Erlbaum.

Benjamin, L. A., & Lord, J. (1996). *Family literacy.* Washington, DC: Office of Education Research and Improvement.

Blakeslee, S. (2005, October 29). Scientists tie two additional genes to dyslexia. *New York Times.* Retrieved April 29, 2007, from www.nytimes.com/2005/10/29/science/29gene.html? pagewanted=print. *New York Times.*

Blakeslee, S. (1991, September 15). Study ties dyslexia to brain flaw affecting vision and other senses. *New York Times,* 1, 30–31.

Bloomfield, L. (1942). Linguistics and reading. *Elementary English Review,* 19, 125–130; 183–186.

Blumenthal, R. (2006, January 13). Houston ties teachers' pay to test scores. *New York Times.* Retrieved April 29, 2007, from www.nytimes.com/2006/01/13/national/13houston.html

Bracey, G. W. (2006). The 16th Bracey report on the condition of public education. *Phi Delta Kappan, 78*(2), 151–166.

Bradsby, S., Wise, J., Mundell, S., & Haas, S. (1992). Making a difference for L.D. students: Matching reading instruction to reading styles through recorded books. *Research in the Classroom,* ED 347 765.

Braio, A., Dunn, R., Beasley, M. T., Quinn, P., & Buchanan, K. (1997). Incremental implementation of learning style strategies among urban low achievers. *Journal of Educational Research, 91,* 15–25.

Bridge, C. A., Winograd, P. N., & Haley, D. (1983). Using predictable materials vs. pre-primers to teach beginning sight words. *The Reading Teacher, 36,* 884–91.

Brooks, J. D. (1991). *Teaching to identified learning styles: The effects upon oral and silent reading and listening comprehension.* Doctoral dissertation, University of Toledo.

Bruner, C. E., & Majewski, W. S. (1990). Mildly handicapped students can succeed with learning styles. *Educational Leadership, 48,* 21–23.

Buechler, M. (2002, February 12). In a letter from the Northwest Educational Laboratory and the National Clearinghouse for Comprehensive School Reform to Marie Carbo at the National Reading Styles Institute, www.nrsi.com.

Burke, K., Guastello, F., Dunn, R., Griggs, S. A., Beasley, T. M., Gemake, J., Sinatra, R., & Lewthwaite, B. (1999–2000). Relationship(s) between global-format and analytic-format learning-style assessments based on the Dunn and Dunn Model. *National Forum of Applied Educational Research Journal, 13*(1), 76–96.

Burton, E. (1980). *An analysis of the interaction of field independence/field dependence and word type as they affect word recognition among kindergartners.* Doctoral dissertation, St. John's University, New York.

Caine, R. N., Caine, G., McClintic, C., & Klimek, K. (2005). *12 brain/mind learning principles in action.* Thousand Oaks, CA: Corwin Press.

Caine, R. N., & Caine, G. (1994). *Making connections: Teaching and the human brain.* New York: Innovative Learning.

Caine, R. S. & Norwood, M. C. (2000). Style preferences make a difference. *The School Administrator, 57*(1), 36.

Carbo, M. (2005). What principals need to know about reading instruction. *Principal, 85*(1), 46–49.

Carbo, M. (1998). The power of reading styles: Accommodating Students' Strengths. In *Perspectives on Reading Instruction.* Alexandria, VA: Association for Supervision and Curriculum Development (pp. 23–26).

Carbo, M. (1997a). Reading styles times twenty. *Educational Leadership, 54*(6), 38–42.

Carbo, M. (1997b). Learning styles strategies that help at-risk students succeed. *Reaching Today's Youth, 1*(2), 37–42.

Carbo, M. (1997c). *What every principal should know about teaching reading.* Syosset, NY: National Reading Styles Institute, Inc.

Carbo, M. (1995). Strategies for increasing achievement in reading. In Robert W. Cole (Ed.), *Educating everybody's children: Diverse strategies for diverse Learners. What research and practice say about improving achievement* (pp. 75–98). Alexandria, VA: Association for Supervision and Curriculum Development.

Carbo, M. (1992). Eliminating the need for dumbed-down textbooks. *Educational Horizons, 70*(4), 189–93.

Carbo, M. (1992) *Reading Style Inventory*® (revised). Roslyn Heights, NY: National Reading Styles Institute.

Carbo, M. (1989). *How to record books for maximum reading gains.* Roslyn, NY: National Reading Styles Institute.

Carbo, M. (1987). Reading styles research: What works isn't always phonics. *Phi Delta Kappan, 68*(6), 431–35.

Carbo, M. (1984). Why most reading tests aren't fair. *Early years pre-K-8, 14*(8), 80–83.

Carbo, M. (1983). Research in reading and learning style: Implications for exceptional children. *Exceptional Children, 49*(6), 486–94.

Carbo, M. (1982) *Reading style inventory.* Roslyn Heights, NY: National Reading Styles Institute.

Carbo, M. (1978a). How to make books talk to children. *The Reading Teacher, 32*(3), 267–73.

Carbo, M. (1978b). A word imprinting technique for children with severe memory disorders. *Teaching Exceptional Children, 11,* 3–5.

Carbo, M., Dunn, R. & Dunn, K. (1991). *Teaching students to read through their individual learning styles.* Boston, MA: Allyn & Bacon.

Carbo Reading Styles Program: Research update (2000). Syosset, NY: National Reading Styles Institute.

Catalog of school reform models, 4th edition (2006). Produced by the Northwest Regional Educational Laboratory and the National Clearinghouse for Comprehensive School Reform. Retrieved April 29, 2007, from www.nwrel.org/scpd/catalog/index.shtml/

Catalog of school reform models, 3rd edition (2002). Produced by the Northwest Regional Educational Laboratory and the National Clearinghouse for Comprehensive School Reform. Retrieved April 29, 2007, from www.nwrel.org/scpd/catalog/index.shtml/

Catalog of school reform models, 2nd edition (1998). Produced by the Northwest Regional Educational Laboratory and the National Clearinghouse for Comprehensive School Reform. Retrieved April 29, 2007, from www.nwrel.org/scpd/catalog/index.shtml/

Chan, L. K. S., Robinson, G. L. W. (1989). The effects of comprehension monitoring instruction for reading disabled students with and without tinted lenses. *Australian Journal of Special Education, 42*(1), 4–13.

Chomsky, C. (1978). When you still can't read in third grade after decoding, what? *Language Arts, 53*(3), 288–96.

Cipielewski, J., & Stanovich, K. (1992). Predicting growth in reading ability from children's exposure to print. *Journal of Experimental Child Psychology, 54,* 74–89.

Clarke, L. K. (1989). Encouraging invented spelling in first-graders' writing: Effects on learning to spell and read. *Research in the Teaching of English, 22,* 281–309.

Coles, G. (2004). Danger in the classroom: "Brain glitch" research and learning to read. Phi Delta Kappan, *85*(5), 344–351.

Coles, G. (2001). Reading taught to the tune of the "scientific" hickory stick. *Phi Delta Kappan, 85,* 205–12.

Coles, G. (2000). *Misreading reading: The bad science that hurts children.* Portsmouth, NH: Heinemann.

Corn, J. (2006). A tale of unintended consequences. *Educational Leadership, 64*(3), 74–78.

Cunningham, P. & Hall, D. (1998). The four blocks: A balanced framework for literacy in primary classrooms. In K. R. Harris, S. Graham, & D. Deshler, (Eds.), *Teaching every child every day: Learning in diverse schools and classrooms.* Cambridge, MA: Brookline Books.

Cunningham, P. M. (1991). *Phonics they use.* New York: Harper Collins.

DeBello, T. (1990). Comparison of eleven major learning styles models: Variables, appropriate populations, validity of instrumentation, and the research behind them. *Journal of Reading, Writing, and Learning Disabilities International, 6,* 203–222.

Defior, S., & Tudela, P. (1994). Effect of phonological training on reading and writing acquisition. *Reading and Writing, 6,* 299–320.

Della Valle, J. (1984). An experimental investigation of the word recognition scores of seventh grade students to provide supervisory and administrative guidelines for the organization of effective instructional environments. (Doctoral dissertation, St. John's University, 1984). *Dissertation Abstracts International, 45,* 359A.

Dillon, S. (2006, September 23). Report says education officials violated rules. *New York Times.* Retrieved April 29, 2007, from www.nytimes.com/2006/09/23/education/23education.html?_r=1&oref=slogin

Dillon, S. (2005a, October 20). Education law gets first test in U.S. schools. *New York Times.* Retrieved April 29, 2007, from www.nytimes.com/2005/10/20/national/20exam.html

Dillon, S. (2005b, December 16). Literacy falls for graduates from college, testing finds. *New York Times.* Retrieved April 29, 2007, from www.nytimes.com/2005/12/16/education/16literacy.html

Dillon, S. (2005c, February 23). Bipartisan study assails no child left behind act. *New York Times.* Retrieved April 29, 2007, from www.nytimes.com/2005/02/23/education/23cnd-child.html

Dillon, S. (2005d, August 22). Connecticut takes U. S. to court over Bush education initiative. *New York Times* Retrieved April 29, 2007, from www.nytimes.com/2005/08/22/nyregion/22cnd-child.html

Dowhower, S. L. (1991). Speaking of prosody: Fluency's unattended bedfellow. *Theory in Practice, 30*(3), 158–164.

Duhaney, L. M. G., & Ewing, N. J. (1998). An investigation of the reading styles of Urban Jamaican middle-grade students with learning disabilities. *Reading Improvement, 35*(3), 114–19.

Duke, N. K. (2000). For the rich it's richer: Print experiences and environments offered to children in very low- and very high-socioeconomic status first-grade classrooms. *American Educational Research Journal, 37*(2), 441–478.

Dunn, R., & DeBello, T. C. (Eds.) (1999). *Improved test scores, attitudes, and behaviors in America's schools: Supervisors' success stories.* Westport, CT: Bergin & Garvey.

Dunn, R., & Griggs, S. A. (2003, 2004). *Synthesis of the Dunn and Dunn learning-style model research: Who, what, when where, and so what?* Jamaica, NY: St. John's University's Center for the Study of Learning and Teaching Styles.

Dunn, R., Griggs, S. A., Olson, J., Gorman, B. & Beasley, M. (1995). A meta-analytic validation of the Dunn and Dunn model of learning style preference. *Journal of Educational Research, 88*, 353–361.

Dunn, R., Della Valle, J., Dunn, K. Geisert, G., Sinatra, R., & Zenhausern, R. (1986). The effects of matching and mismatching students' mobility preferences on recognition and memory tasks. *Journal of Educational Research, 79*, 262–272.

Dunn, R., & Dunn, K. (1999). *The complete guide to the learning styles in-service system.* Boston: Allyn & Bacon.

Dunn, R., & Dunn, K. (1998). *Practical approaches to individualizing staff development for adults.* Westport, CT: Praeger.

Dunn, R., & Dunn, K. (2005). Thirty-five years of research on perceptual strengths. *The Clearing House, 78*(6), 273–276.

ECS's programs & practices. (2002, February 13). Denver, CO: Education Commission of the States.

Elliot, I. (1991). The reading place. *Teaching K-8, 21*(3), 3034.

Fair, S. (1982). *The bedspread.* New York, NY: William Morrow & Company.

Fels, C. (1993). *Rose and tulip.* Syosset, NY: National Reading Styles Institute, Inc.

Fernald, G. (1943). *Remedial techniques in basic school subjects.* New York: McGraw-Hill.

Flick, G. L. (1996). *Power parenting for children with ADD/ADHD: A practical parents' guide for managing difficult behaviors.* Nyack, NY: Center for Applied Research in Education.

Flippo, R. F. (1998). Points of agreement: A display of professional unity in our field. *The Reading Teacher, 52*, 30–40.

Foertsch, M.A. (1992). *Reading in and out of school: Factors influencing the literacy achievement of American students in grades 4, 8, and 12, in 1988 and 1990.* Washington, DC: Office of Educational Research and Improvement.

Ford, D. (1996). *Reversing underachievement among gifted black students.* New York: Teachers College Press.

Friedman, T. L. (2005). *The world is flat: A brief history of the twenty-first century.* New York: Farrar, Straus, and Giroux.

Fries, C. C. (1962). *Linguistics and reading.* New York: Holt, Rinehart, and Winston.

Frymier, J., Barber, L., Carriedo, R., Denton, W., Gansneder, B., Johnson-Lewis., & Robertson, N. (1992). *Final report—Phi delta kappa students at risk, Volume 1.*

Growing up is risky business and schools are not to blame. Bloomington, IN: Phi Delta Kappa.

Gaskins, I. W., Downer, M. A., Anderson, R. C., Cunningham, P. M., Gaskins, R. W., Schommer, M., & the Teachers of Benchmark School. (1988). A meta-cognitive approach to phonics: Using what you know to decode what you don't know. *Remedial and Special Education, 9,* 36–41.

Gaspard, J. (2006). In an e-mail to Juliet DiTroia, June 18, 2006.

Gibbons, P. (1991). *Learning to learn in a second language.* Newtown, Australia: Heinemann.

Gilbert, A. G. (1977). *Teaching the three r's through movement experiences.* Englewood Cliffs, NJ: Prentice Hall.

Gilliam, B., Gerla, J. P., & Wright, G. (2004). Providing minority parents with relevant literacy activities for their children. *Reading Improvement, 41*(4), 226–234.

Gillingham, A., & Stillman, B. (1968). *Remedial teaching for children with specific disability in reading, spelling and penmanship.* Cambridge, MA: Educator's Publishing Service.

Goodman K. S & Goodman, Y. (1979). Learning to read is natural. *Theory and Practice of Early Reading,* Volume 1, pp. 137–154. Mahwah, NJ: Lawrence Erlbaum Associates.

Gorman, C. (2003, July 28). The new science of dyslexia. *Time,* 52–59.

Greer, E. (2002, March 5). Implications for a scientific-based evidence approach in reading. U. S. Department of Education, Retrieved April 29, 2007, from www.ed.gov/nclb/research/greer.html

Guthrie, J. T., Schafer, W. D., & Huang, C. (2001). Benefits of opportunity to read and balanced instruction on the NAEP. *The Journal of Educational Research, 94*(3), 145–162.

Hannaford, C. (1995). *Smart moves—Why learning is not all in your head.* Arlington, VA: Great Ocean Publishers.

Hart, L. (1983). Programs, patterns, and downshifting in learning to read. *The Reading Teacher, 37,* 4–11.

Heckelman, R. G. (1969). A neurological-impress method of remedial reading instruction. *Academic Therapy Quarterly, 4*(4), 277–82.

Henson-Parker, D. (2005). *See it Right!® (short form manual).* Rancho Cucamonga, CA: See it Right!® Corporation.

Henson-Parker, D. (2003a). *See it Right!® training video.* Rancho Cucamonga, CA: See it Right!® Corporation.

Henson-Parker, D. (2003b). *See it Right!® awareness video.* Rancho Cucamonga, CA: See it Right!® Corporation.

Henson-Parker, D. (1997). Diagnosis and remediation of visual perceptual problems by the use of colored transparencies—a new approach. *International School Psychology XXth Annual Colloquium Proceedings,* 136–139. Paper available at www.seeitright.com

Hiebert, E. H., Pearson, P. D., Taylor, B. M., Richardson, V., & Paris, S. G. (1998). Early concepts: Concepts of print, letter naming, and phonemic awareness. In *Every child a reader: Applying reading research in the classroom* (Topic 2 in the series). Ann Arbor, MI: University of Michigan School of Education, Center for the Improvement of Early Reading Achievement.

Hiebert, E. H., & Raphael, T. E. (1998). *Early reading instruction.* New York: Harcourt Brace.

Hodgin, J., & Wooliscroft, C. (1997). Eric learns to read: Learning styles at work. *Educational Leadership, 54*(6), 43–45.

Hoffman, J. V. (1987). Rethinking the role of oral reading. *Elementary School Journal, 87,* 367–373.

Holdaway, D. (1979). *The foundations of literacy.* Sydney: Ashton-Scholastic.

Hudson, R. F., High, L., & Al Otaiba, S. (2007). Dyslexia and the brain: What does current research tell us? *The Reading Teacher, 60*(6), 506–515.

Hudson, R. F., Lane, H. B., & Pullen, P. C. (2005). Reading fluency assessment and instruction: What, why, and how? *The Reading Teacher, 58*(8), 702–714.

International Reading Association. (2000). *Making a difference means making it different: Honoring children's rights to excellent reading instruction.* Barksdale, DE: Author.

IRA responds to report on Reading First. (2006, October/November). *Reading Today, 24*(2), 1, 3.

Irlen H. (1991). *Reading by the colors: Overcoming dyslexia and other reading disabilities through the Irlen method.* Garden City Park, NY: Avery Publishing Group, Inc.

Jensen, E. (1998a). *Introduction to brain compatible learning.* Thousand Oaks, CA: Corwin Press.

Jensen, E. (1998b). *Teaching with the brain in mind.* Alexandria, VA: Association for Curriculum and Development.

Johnston, F. R. (1999). The timing and teaching of word families. *The Reading Teacher, 53*(1), 64–75.

Johnston, P., & Allington, R. (1991). Remediation. In R. Barr, M. L. Kamil, P. Mosenthal, & P. D. Pearson (Eds.), *Handbook of reading research: Volume II* (pp. 984–1012). White Plains, NY: Longman.

Killion, J. (2002a, October 21). In a letter on behalf of the National Staff Development Council and the National Education Association to Marie Carbo at the National Reading Styles Institute.

Killion, J. (2002b). *What works in the elementary school: Results-based staff development* (pp. 48–51) Oxford, OH: National Staff Development Council.

Koskinea, P. S., Blum, I. H., Bisson, S. A., Phillips, S. M., Creamer, T. S., & Baker, T. K. (1999). Shared reading, books, and audio tapes: Supporting diverse students in school and at home. *The Reading Teacher, 52*(8), 430–444.

Kozol, J. (2005). Confections of apartheid: A stick-and-carrot pedagogy for the children of our inner-city poor. *Phi Delta Kappan, 87*(4), 264–275.

Krashen, S. (1993). *The power of reading: Insights from the research.* Englewood, CO: Libraries Unlimited.

Krimsky, J. (1982). An analysis of the effects of matching and mismatching fourth grade students with their learning style preference for the environmental element of light and their subsequent reading speed and accuracy scores. (Doctoral dissertation, St. John's University, 1982). *Dissertation Abstracts International, 43,* 66A.

Krugman, P. (2005, July 25). Toyota, moving northward. New York Times. Retrieved April 29, 2007, from www.nytimes.com/2005/07/25/opinion/25krugman.html

LaBerge, D., & Samuels, S. J. (1974). Toward a theory of automatic information processing in reading. *Cognitive Psychology, 6,* 293–323.

LaShell, L. (1986). *An analysis of the effects of reading methods upon reading achievement and locus of control when individual reading style is matched for learning-disabled students.* Doctoral Dissertation, Fielding University.

Levin, H., & Holmes, N. (2005, November 7). America's learning deficit, *The New York Times*, A25.

List of promising practices in reading (2000). Denver, CO: Education Commission of the States.

Livingstone, M. S., Rosen, G. D., Drislane, F. W., Galaburda, A. M. (1991). Physiological and anatomical evidence for a magnocellular defect in developmental dyslexia. *Neurobiology, 88*, 7943–7947.

Manzo, K. K. (1998, March 25). NRC panel urges end to reading wars: Scholars suggest multiple approaches. *Education Week, 1*, 18.

Martin, J. (1996). *Sight words that stick*. Syosset, NY: National Reading Styles Institute.

McKeown, M. G. (1993). Creating effective definitions for young word learners. *Reading Research Quarterly, 28*, 16–31.

Miller, G.A., & Gildea, P.M. (1987). How children learn words. *Scientific American, 257*(3), 94–99.

Mohrmann, S. R. (1990). *Learning styles of poor readers*. Paper presented at the annual conference of the Southwest Educational Research Association, Austin, Texas.

Molbeck, C. H. (1994). Using recorded books with reluctant readers. *WSRA Journal, 38*(2), 39–42.

Moorman, M., & Turner, M. (1999). What Johnny likes to read is hard to find in school. *Reading Research Quarterly, 34*(1), 12–27.

Morris, B. (2003, February 1). In an e-mail message to Linda Queiruga.

Morris, D., & Nelson, L. (1992). Supported oral reading and low achieving second graders. *Reading Research and Instruction, 32*, 49–63.

Nagy, W. E., & Scott, J. A. (2000). Vocabulary processes. In M. L. Kamil, P. B. Mosenthal, P. D. Pearson, & R. Barr (Eds.), *Handbook of reading research: Vol. III* (pp. 269–284). Mahwah, NJ: Erlbaum.

Nagy, W. E., Anderson, R. C., & Herman, P. A. (1987). Learning word meanings from context during normal reading. *American Educational Research Journal, 24*(2), 237–270.

Nagy, W. E., Herman, P. A., & Anderson, R. C. (1985). Learning words from context, *Reading Research Quarterly, 20*(2), 233–253.

Nagy, W. E., & Anderson, R. C. (1984). How many words are there in printed school English? *Reading Research Quarterly, 19*, 304–330.

National Reading Panel (2000). *Teaching children to read: An evidence-based assessment of the scientific research literature on reading and its implications for reading instruction—Reports of the subgroups*. Washington, DC: National Institute of Child Health and Human Development. Retrieved April 29, 2007, from www.nationalreadingpanel.org

Neuman, S. B., Caperelli, B. J., & Kee, C. (1998). Literacy learning, a family matter. *The Reading Teacher, 52*, 244–252.

Newkirk, T. (2003, September 10). The quiet crisis in boys' literacy. Retrieved April 29, 2007, from www.edweek.org/ew/articles/2003/09/10/02newkirk.h23.html?querystring=comic%20books&print=1

O'Connor, P. D., Sofo, F., Kendall, L., & Olsen, G. (1990). Reading disabilities and the effect of coloured filters. *Journal of Learning Disabilities, 23*(10), 597–603, 620.

Oexle, J. E., & Zenhausern, R. (1981). Differential hemispheric activation in good and poor readers. *International Journal of Neuroscience, 51*, 31–36.

Oglesby, F., & Suter, W. N. (1995). Matching reading styles and reading instruction. *Research in the Schools* (2005, December 7), 2(1), 11–15.

Olson, L. (December 7, 2005). Nationwide standards eyed anew. *Education Week, 25*(14), 1, 24.

Orton, S. T. (1937). *Reading, writing, and speech problems in children.* New York: W. W. Norton & Co., Inc.

Pappas, C. C. (1993). Is narrative primary? Some insights from kindergarteners' pretend readings of stories and information books. *Journal of Reading Behavior, 25*(1), 97–129.

Parker, M. (October 20, 2005). Photon induced visual abnormalities (PIVAA) and visual dyslexia. Closing the Gap Conference, Minneapolis, MN.

Pearson, P. D., & Camperell, K. (1994). Comprehension of text structures. In R. B. Ruddell, M. R. Ruddell, & H. Singer (Eds.), *Theoretical models and processes of reading* (4th ed., pp. 448–468). Newark, DE: International Reading Association.

Pearson, P. D. (1992). Reading. In M. C. Alkin (Ed.), *Encyclopedia of educational research: Volume III* (pp. 1075–1085). New York: Macmillan.

Perfetti, C. A. (1985). *Reading ability.* New York: Oxford University Press.

Pizzo, J. (1981). An investigation of the relationships between selected acoustic environments and sound, an element of learning style, as they affect sixth-grade students reading achievement and attitudes. (Doctoral dissertation, St. John's University, 1984). *Dissertation Abstracts International, 46,* 342A.

Prell, P. A. (1986). Improving test scores—Teaching test wiseness: A Review of the Literature. *Phi Delta Kappa Research Bulletin, No. 5.* Bloomington, IN: Phi Delta Kappa, Center on Evaluation, Development, and Research.

Pressley, M. (2001). *Effective beginning reading instruction.* Chicago, National Reading Conference.

Pressley, M. (1998). *Reading instruction that works: The case for balanced teaching.* New York: Guilford.

Queiruga, L. (1992). *Saving potential dropouts with the Carbo Reading Styles Program.* Paper presented at the Eighth National Reading Styles Conference. Available upon request to NRSI, Box 737, Syosset, NY 11791.

Rasmussen, D., & Goldberg, L. (1964). *A pig can jig.* Chicago: Science Research Associates.

Ravitch, D. (2005, November 7). Every state left behind. *The New York Times.* Retrieved April 29, 2007, from www.nytimes.com/2005/11/07/opinion/07 ravitch.html

Renzulli, J. S. (1994). *Schools for talent development.* Mansfield Center, CT: Creative Learning Press.

Research on the Dunn and Dunn Model. (2000). Jamaica, NY: St. John's University's Center for the Study of Learning and Teaching Styles.

Results-based practices showcase. (1997–1998). Louisville, KY: Kentucky Department of Education, Division of School Improvement.

Reutzel, D. R. & Smith, J. A. (2004). Accelerating struggling readers' progress: A comparative analysis of expert opinion and current research recommendations. *Reading & Writing Quarterly, 20,* 63–89.

Reutzel, D. R., Hollingsworth, P. M., & Eldredge, L. (1994). Oral reading instruction: The impact on student reading development. *Reading Research Quarterly, 29,* 40–62.

Reutzel, D. R., & Hollingsworth, P. M. (1993). Effects of fluency training on second graders' reading comprehension. *Journal of Educational Research, 86,* 325–331.

Rief, S. F. (1993). *How to reach and teach ADD/ADHD children.* West Nyack, NY: Center for Applied Research in Education.

Roberts, A. V. (1998/1999). Effects of tactual and kinesthetic instructional methods on social-studies achievement and attitude test scores of fifth-grade students. *National Forum of Teacher Education Journal, 9*(1), 16–26.

Robinson, G. L. W., & Conway, R. N. F. (1990). The effects of Irlen coloured lenses on specific reading skills and perception of ability: a twelve-month validity study. *Journal of Learning Disabilities, 23*(10), 588–597.

Samuels, S. J. (1988). Decoding and automaticity: Helping poor readers become automatic at word recognition. *The Reading Teacher, 41*, 756–60.

Schacter, J. (2000). *Reading programs that work: A review of programs for pre- kindergarten to 4th grade*. Santa Monica, CA: Milken Family Foundation.

Schemo, D. J., & Fessenden, F. (December 3, 2003). Gains in Houston schools: How real are they? *New York Times*. Retrieved April 29, 2007, from www.nytimes .com/2006/01/13/national/13houston.html?pagewanted=print

Sharmat, M. (1980). *Gregory, the terrible eater*. New York: Scholastic, Inc.

Shaywitz, S. E., Shaywitz, B. A., Pugh, K. R. Fulbright, R. K., Constable, R. T., Mencl, W. E., Shankweiler, D. P., Lieberman, A. M., Skudlarski, P., Fletcher, J. M., Katz, L., Marchione, K. E., Lacadie, C., Gatenby, C., & Gore, J. C. (1998). Functional disruption in the organization of the brain for reading in dyslexia. *Proceedings of the National Academy of Sciences, 95*, 2636–41.

Shea, T. C. (1983). An investigation of the relationship among preferences for the learning style element of design, selected instructional environments, and reading achievement with ninth grade students to improve administrative determinations concerning effective educational facilities. (Doctoral dissertation, St. John's University). *Dissertation Abstracts International, 44*, 2004A.

Simpson, C. (2001). *Copyright for schools: A practical guide* (3rd ed). Worthington, OH: Linworth Publishing, Inc.

Skipper, B. (1997). Reading with style. *American School Board Journal, 184*(2), 36–37.

Slavin, R. E., & Cheung, A. (2004). *A synthesis of research on language of reading instruction for English language learners*. Institute of Education Sciences. U.S. Department of Education (Grant No. OERI-R-117–40005).

Smith, M. W., & Wilhelm, J. D. (2002). *Reading don't fix no Chevys: Literacy in the lives of young men*. Portsmouth, NH: Heinemann.

Snyder, A. E. (1994). On the road to reading recovery. *The School Administrator, 51*(1), 23–24.

Snyder, A. E. (1997). Utilization of a systemic design and learning styles model as a paradigm for restructuring education. Doctoral Dissertation, Tennessee State University, Nashville.

Spangenberg-Urbschat, K., & Pritchard, R. (1994). *Kids come in all languages: Reading instruction for ESL students*. Newark, DE: International Reading Association.

Sprenger, M. (2003). *Differentiation through learning styles and memory*. Thousand Oaks, CA: Corwin Press, Inc.

Sprenger, M. (1999). *Learning and memory: The brain in action*. Alexandria, VA: Association for Supervision and Curriculum Development.

Stahl, S. A., Duffy-Hester, A. M., & Stahl, K. A. D. (1998). Everything you wanted to know about phonics (but were afraid to ask). *Reading Research Quarterly, 33*(3), 338–355.

Stahl, S. (1992). Saying the "p" word. Nine guidelines for exemplary phonics instruction. *The Reading Teacher, 45*, 618–25.

Stanovich, K. E. (2000). Progress in understanding reading: Some consequences of individual differences in the acquisition of literacy. *Reading Research Quarterly, 21*(4), 360–407.

Stanovich, K. E. (1980). Toward an interactive-compensatory model of individual differences in the development of reading fluency. *Reading Research Quarterly, 16*, 32–71.

Sternberg, R. J. (1987). Most vocabulary is learned from context. In M. G. McKeown & M. E. Curtis (Eds.), *The nature of vocabulary acquisition* (pp. 89–105). Hillsdale, NJ: Erlbaum.

Strickland, D. (2007). *Teaching phonics today: A primer for educators.* Newark, DE: International Reading Association.

Sudzina, M. (1993). *An investigation of the relationship between the reading styles of second-graders and their achievement in three basal reader treatments.* (ERIC Document Reproduction Service No. ED 353 569).

Swanborn, M. S. L., & de Glopper, K. (1999). Incidental word learning while reading: A meta-analysis. *Review of Educational Research, 69*(3), 261–285.

Szabo, L. (2006). ADHD treatment is getting a workout. *USA Today*, Life Section, D6. Retrieved April 29, 2007, http://pqasb.pqarchiver.com/USAToday/access/1010674161.html?dids=1010674161:1010674161&FMT=ABS&FMTS=ABS:FT&date=Mar+27%2C+2006&author=Liz+Szabo&pub=USA+TODAY&edition=&startpage=D.6&desc=ADHD+treatment+is+getting+a+workout

Tendy, S. M., & Geiser, W. F. (1998–99). The search for style: It all depends on where you look. *National Forum of Teacher Education Journal, 9*(1), 3–15.

Thies, A. P. (1999/2000). The neuropsychology of learning styles. *National Forum of Applied Educational Research Journal, 13*(1), 50–62.

Thomasson, R. (1993). *Patterns for hands-on learning.* Syosset, NY: National Reading Styles Institute.

Toppo, G. (2005, October 20). Math proficiency rises, but reading stagnates. *USA Today*, 7D.

Trelease, J. (2006). *The read-aloud handbook.* (6th ed.). New York: Penguin.

Tyre, P. (2006, January 30). The trouble with boys. Retrieved April 29, 2007, from www.msnbc.msn.com/id/10965522/site/newsweek/print/1/displaymode/1098/

Walker, S. Y. (1994). *The survival guide for parents of gifted kids.* Minneapolis: Free Spirit Publishing Co.

Winebrenner, S. (1992). *Teaching gifted kids in the regular classroom.* Minneapolis: Free Spirit Publishing Co.

Wilson, I. G. (1993). *Reading styles of Hispanic students with learning disabilities in third, fourth and fifth grade.* Doctoral dissertation, University of Miami.

Wunderlich, K. C. (1988). *A teacher's guide to behavioral interventions: Intervention strategies for behavior problems in the educational environment.* Columbia, MO: Hawthorne Educational Services.

Yopp, H. K. (1995). Read-aloud books for developing phonemic awareness: An annotated bibliography. *The Reading Teacher, 48*, 538–543.

Index

CORWIN PRESS

The Corwin Press logo—a raven striding across an open book—represents the union of courage and learning. Corwin Press is committed to improving education for all learners by publishing books and other professional development resources for those serving the field of PreK–12 education. By providing practical, hands-on materials, Corwin Press continues to carry out the promise of its motto: **"Helping Educators Do Their Work Better."**

NAESP

NATIONAL ASSOCIATION OF ELEMENTARY SCHOOL PRINCIPALS

Serving All Elementary and Middle Level Principals

The 29,500 members of the National Association of Elementary School Principals provide administrative and instructional leadership for public and private elementary and middle schools throughout the United States, Canada, and overseas. Founded in 1921, NAESP is today a vigorously independent professional association with its own headquarters building in Alexandria, Virginia, just across the Potomac River from the nation's capital. From this special vantage point, NAESP conveys the unique perspective of the elementary and middle school principal to the highest policy councils of our national government. Through national and regional meetings, award-winning publications, and joint efforts with its 50 state affiliates, NAESP is a strong advocate both for its members and for the 33 million American children enrolled in preschool, kindergarten, and grades 1 through 8.